DON'T BUY IT

DON'T BUY IT

The Trouble with Talking Nonsense
About the Economy

ANAT SHENKER-OSORIO

PUBLICAFFAIRS
New York

Published in the United States by PublicAffairs™, a Member of the Perseus Books Group

All rights reserved.
Printed in the United States of America.

Passages of chapter 4 first appeared in the *Christian Science Monitor*, April 4, 2011. Passages that appear in chapter 6 were originally published in "Life Is Not a Zero-Sum Game," Huffington Post, March 10, 2010.

PublicAffairs books are available at special discounts for bulk purchases in the U.S. by corporations, institutions, and other organizations. For more information, please contact the Special Markets Department at the Perseus Books Group, 2300 Chestnut Street, Suite 200, Philadelphia, PA 19103, call (800) 810-4145, ext. 5000, or e-mail special.markets@perseusbooks.com.

Text design by Jeff Williams

Library of Congress Cataloging-in-Publication Data
Shenker-Osorio, Anat.
    Don't buy it : the trouble with talking nonsense about the economy / Anat Shenker-Osorio. — 1st ed.
        p. cm.
    Includes bibliographical references and index.
    ISBN 978-1-61039-177-1 (hbk. : alk. paper) — ISBN 978-1-61039-178-8 (e-book)
1. United States—Economic conditions—2009– 2. United States—Economic policy—2009– 3. Economics. I. Title.

HC106.84.S54 2012
330.973—dc23
                                                                                2012022519
First Edition

10 9 8 7 6 5 4 3 2 1

To my fellow Madisonians

Contents

Preface

A False Idol

Thou shalt have no other gods before me.
—EXODUS 20:3

Many of us are daily left wondering how to make sense of the contradictions we personally experience and hear about the economy. The news tells us the recession ended in 2009, but unemployment has proven stubbornly stable. Pundits contend we've seen the end of the housing bubble, but home prices in most places won't budge and foreclosures continue. Our growth rate has registered positive since the summer of 2009, but poverty levels are also on the rise. What's going on, what will happen next, and how do we even begin to make sense of the economy?

I'm here to save you some boring. There's no need to actually read long economic treatises, sit through lectures, or decipher expensive textbooks; you don't even have to bother scrutinizing the graphs on the *Wall Street Journal* business page to learn what's going on right now with the U.S. economy. It's simpler than you think: all you need to know about the economy you can get from cartoons—a single show, in fact.

In their magnum opus, "Margaritaville," season 13, episode 3, *South Park* creators Trey Parker and Matt Stone have done us a service, revealing over the course of twenty-two animated minutes what it might otherwise take several semesters at a decent business school to learn. The episode opens in the small Colorado town of South Park, which is wracked by a sudden and serious economic decline. After a period of collective soul-searching, the locals hit upon the obvious cause of rampant unemployment and plummeting stock values: the Economy is pissed.

The citizens cower upon realizing the truth—the Economy is an angry and vengeful God. Because South Parkers have paid insufficient homage to it, the Economy visits ruination and recession upon them. A character lectures a crowd of rapt listeners, "There are those who will say the Economy has forsaken us. Nay! You have forsaken the Economy. And now you know the Economy's wrath."

The solution in South Park, as will be familiar to modern-day Greeks and low-income Americans, is sacrifice. The cartoon version of this goes full throttle: Bible-inspired acts of piety and prostration ensue. Citizens turn their sheets into togas and cease to buy or sell things altogether in an attempt to show deference before the Economy.

"Sacrifice" is not an arbitrary or accidental word choice. It's become a hallowed term in our national lexicon, the preferred prescription for achieving propitious economic results. Minus the dead animals and altars, politicians, pundits, and peddlers of conventional wisdom have asked us to sacrifice over and over again. In 2010, *Washington Post* columnist David Broder wrote that "everyone and every institution will have to contribute—no, *genuinely, sacrifice*—if we are to repair the damage to our economic health."[1] GOP presidential contender Mitt Romney admonished, "My plan for America requires real leadership—and *it calls for sacrifice*. It does not require a leader to promise bigger and bigger benefits and something for nothing. It requires a leader to call for sacrifice."[2] When Senator Tom Coburn (R-OK) outlined his plan to cut spending, he remarked, "There will not be one American that will not be *called to sacrifice*."[3] They may not be asking us to pull on hair shirts or flagellate ourselves with whips, but their high praise of austerity as solution rings sadly true to South Park's notion of Economy as deity.

Deity isn't the only form our economy takes in popular perception. In current discourse about economic policy and in prevailing explanations of events, it has become all too common to treat the economy as a living, breathing, intentional being. One that by all means we should avoid *hurting*. You can likely recall hearing on TV or reading in the news some variation on "We can't do [fill in socially beneficial act] because it will *hurt* the economy." Or, "If we do [thing that will make Americans' lives better], it will *scare* the markets."

In 2011, Representative Jeb Hensarling (R-TX) warned, "Increasing tax revenues could *hurt the economy*."[4] House Speaker John Boehner (R-OH) and Representative Eric Cantor (R-VA) echoed his sentiments in a *USA Today* op-ed:

"With nervous markets, . . . the worst thing Washington can do *for our economy* is raise taxes on the people we need to start hiring again."[5] Conservative think tank the Heritage Foundation has long preached that unemployment benefits damage the economy.[6]

Other things that supposedly give the economy apoplexy? Take your pick: regulations, welfare programs, government spending, helping the poor, raindrops on roses and whiskers on kittens.

But when was the last time you heard a discussion about whether a potential policy might hurt, harm, weaken, or threaten *people*? Americans like you and me. Instead, we've been taught to be so preoccupied with the abstract fate and feelings of the economy that what happens to us doesn't even enter into the discussion.

Other issues of national concern don't evidence such rhetorical treatment. Military matters, for example, are generally framed as being vital to protecting our national security interests. No one attempts to justify military action because our armies need to grow or because if we don't start a war, some branch of the military's feelings might be hurt. Military action has to be linked to the good of the American people in any effective sales pitch.

Consider, as another example, how we craft our arguments about education. Whether on the side of vouchers and charters or on the side of unions and addressing disparities, you better believe the people arguing it are characterizing their position as "for the children." This phrase is repeated so often it has become a punch line. But the point is, you won't catch anyone insisting that his or her big education reform idea will further the field of pedagogy itself or contribute mightily to our awareness of child development.

But the "for the people" sales pitch becomes insufficient, or just plain inaudible, whenever talk turns directly to money matters. The American people are admonished to work, consume, and sacrifice to make sure the economy doesn't get grumpy, skittish, or vindictive. In most domains, policies must be advertised as serving our national interests, but when GDP talk rolls around, this is no longer the case. We're here to please the economy, not the other way around.

Our Economy is furthermore billed as a pretty particular deity: an Old Testament style of God. Apparently, insufficient "faith" in it can catalyze disaster. Economists have a special variable to quantify this kind of belief: it's called consumer confidence. We measure it like any other economic indicator; only instead of being an actual tabulation of monies spent, jobs gained, or taxes collected, it tabulates the vague sense of how people feel about what may or may not come to pass.

As we'll learn in subsequent pages, our monetary high priests' readings of the economic Tarot have taken the place of centuries of lived experience, cross-country comparisons, and testable theories. Their say alone can justify policies of austerity and debt reduction peddled to us most often by the right. You've heard of faith-based social initiatives? Welcome to myth-based economics.

With the Economy established as our overlord, the bankers and CEOs who interpret its omnipotent ways can be seen as its ordained intermediaries, presiding in their too-big-to-fail temples. Simple serfs like you and I hand over tithes and tributes in the form of obscure fees, but frustrated as we may get, we don't dare defy the clergy of finance. No matter how naked their greed and obvious their sins, we're scared to topple these people. Without them who would make sense of and pay proper homage to the Economy? The direct line of communication to the almighty dollar is theirs alone.

Like their priestly predecessors, those closest to the Economy dress up in their bespoke Brooks Brother vestments, break all the rules, and tell the rest of us peons to keep our heads down and noses clean and to sacrifice. CEOs' golden parachutes and bankers' bonuses, doled out regardless of performance, make the old-school practice of selling indulgences seem almost quaint. And yet, for fear of upending the established order, making Wall Street less "competitive," and thus enraging the Economy anew, our leaders turn a blind eye. Or, perhaps more aptly, offer a wink and a nod. As of this writing the Justice Department has yet to try a single financial firm executive in criminal court for fraud. Let me clarify—our government hasn't even *tried* to try them. Granted, there have been some civil finger wagging and a few fines that are—considering the riches of the parties involved—little more than chump change.[7]

Some may make the argument that this failure even to attempt to hold top bankers accountable is due simply to the fact that while deeply unethical, their actions were not actually illegal. In other words, they fall under the heading of stupid and crappy but do not extend to violation of our laws. But refusing to even ask the question in court signals just how loathe we are to challenge these mighty men of money.

Mainline thinking about the U.S. economy is starting to resemble Scientology: beyond a coterie of high-profile, high-income believers, the more those of us outside the fold learn about the teachings, the wackier the whole enterprise sounds. Members who attempt to leave either orthodoxy—in one case a church and in the other a market-worship orientation—are shunned and ostracized.

Where once we looked to the weather to indicate how we were tracking with God, now televised market reports tell us hourly how the Economy regards our latest offerings. Whether we have our life savings wrapped up in the stock market or have nothing at all, a bad NASDAQ report today has become as crucial as rainfall quantities were to our ancestors: a serious matter of life or death. You may have no idea what the ten-year T-note is, but hearing that it has fallen as good as assures you there'll be lean times ahead.

The debt clock, the consumer price index, the unemployment report, the latest quarterly earnings—we're bombarded by figures we barely understand that nonetheless profoundly affect how we feel about ourselves and the world. Our hope and our happiness have become intimately tied to abstractions. It's a quick hop from there to getting us to think we're here for the Economy.

In a nutshell, the overriding message is twofold: it's your fault that the Economy sucks, but there's not much you can do to improve it. This storyline must sound achingly familiar to Christians. The blame for damnation to hell lies with you and you alone. Yet though prayer and piety are good ideas, only God determines who merits redemption. Economic salvation is out of your hands, but that's no excuse to quit your night job or start spending on luxury items like college.

HOW DID THIS HAPPEN? How did we come to accept that how well *we're* doing depends entirely on how well *it's* doing? How did we forget the economy is nothing more or less than what we make and consume, nothing outside of *us*?

The answer is neither straightforward nor obvious. History provides us some of the story, but much of what happened lies in our language itself. The prevailing ways people donning the mantle of economic wisdom communicate about the economy—the very metaphors and personifications used regularly to explain its workings—have become not just agents of misinformation but actual tools for increasing and prolonging misfortune. Confuse us enough about what the economy is and how it operates, and we will jump at the chance to do what we are told is its bidding.

What we say, write, and hear about our economy profoundly affects what we expect it to do and how we interact with it. The standard lines—what I'll be referring to as economic discourse and messaging—enable those in power to convince us the only logical course of action is to go without to keep the economy healthy and thriving. This same rhetoric constrains the policy solutions we come up with to meet our needs and hinders what we'll dare to dream could be.

Fealty to a higher power. Admonitions to make do with less while producing more. Sounds like a right-wing sonata in C minor, doesn't it? But while you might be tempted to blame this on the conservative spin machine, notice who else has bought and sold this version of how the economy works. In two words: practically everyone.

You may recall, during the last Democratic administration, Bill Clinton's mantra: "Work hard and play by the rules." In his usage, at least, it was more a statement of what ought to be than a directive to countrymen and -women to get off our butts and start doing. The full phrase from his 1992 campaign was "People who work hard and play by the rules shouldn't be poor."[8] Yet while it may have been intended as a message of well-deserved empathy for working-class Americans, it sprang from the same source of economy worship that today justifies Republicans' push for a new age of austerity.

The quasi commandment "Work hard and play by the rules" has a long and bipartisan history. It may, in fact, be one of the strongest links across the famed political aisle. Geraldine Ferraro (D-NY) was the first to state it on the record, in her 1984 speech accepting the vice presidential nomination at the Democratic National Convention.[9] Governor Arnold Schwarzenegger (R-CA) took up the same theme in 2004, saying, "If you work hard and play by the rules, this country is truly open to you."[10]

Progressive Democrats have taken up this trope as recently as 2011. In that year, Van Jones's Rebuild the Dream, a nonprofit organization dedicated to advocating, among other things, against austerity policies, recycled this tidbit in its introductory manifesto.[11] Rebuild states that the American Dream is based on the idea that "if you work hard and play by the rules, you can live with dignity, provide for your family, and give your kids a better life."[12]

This definition of the American Dream may, in fact, serve as a stirring goal statement. I too believe in the dignity, security, and well-being of all. I begrudge no one a house plus mortgage payment of his or her very own, even if plummeting values mean he or she may need scuba gear to get in the front door. But by admonishing Americans to "work hard and play by the rules," politicians and activists are directing us on a path that's proven untraversable. It doesn't do us or the economy any good. To fully make the case that this phrase is not helping us, let's turn now to consider its component parts.

EXHIBIT A: PLAY BY THE RULES

Playing by the rules is a great principle, until you realize that the rules aren't working for just about 99% of us. First, let's consider just how arbitrary the rules are; they don't necessarily advance us toward desirable outcomes. Just ask Kelley Williams-Boler, a single mother of two from Ohio who was sentenced to jail time for breaking the rules.[13] Her transgression? Using her father's mailing address in lieu of her own in an effort to get her kids into a better school district. The rules had consigned them to one plagued by violence. Formerly a special education teacher's aide, having this felony on her record means she will no longer be eligible for employment in her profession. Even "working hard" is now out of the question for her.

Second, if being irrational weren't enough, the rules are biased. Just ask Lilly Ledbetter, who diligently followed rules for nineteen years at Goodyear Tire, only to find her vagina cutting into her paycheck.[14] Nearing retirement, Ledbetter learned that her male colleagues earned far more than she did for the same work. Although the Supreme Court ruled that she experienced discrimination, it nevertheless threw out her case on a technicality. The claim had not been filed within 180 days of the first instance when Goodyear shortchanged her. Never mind she only learned of the disparity years after it had first occurred.

Third, what about cases where we selectively enforce the rules depending on the day or the purported rule breaker? Ask any one of our 12 million immigrants denied the protections their initiative and labor have earned them. To hear opponents of immigration tell it, they are the biggest rule breakers of all. Forget about the otherwise all-important "hard work" they sunk into making an economic life here. I'd put forth that they are our best illustration of how thoroughly the rules have proven ineffective.

The obvious beneficiaries of these much-hallowed rules seem to be the country club cronies who hang together to ensure all of the rules are applicable only to the rest of us suckers. As political theorist Kevin Carson succinctly puts it, "The only people who get rich playing by the rules are the people who make the rules."[15]

By putting emphasis on playing by the rules, we lend credence and our seal of approval to the prevailing notion that the onus for outcomes must always lie with the individual. Using this phrase, we remain willfully silent about the systems that determine the conditions in which people operate—the many different sets of rules that apply to different groups. The fact is that the incredibly disparate circumstances of birth and institutional and unconscious prejudice in this country—not to mention the social capital that accrues from attending the "right" schools alongside the "right" people—are among the long list of things that guarantee that for some lucky people, the rulebook need never apply. The world works differently for each person depending on race, class, gender, geography, place of birth, and sexual orientation. Yet by using the phrase "play by the rules," we insist on preserving the fantasy that meritocracy determines success in America. Until we reform the rules to apply equally without exception or exclusion—and let's face it, we've never succeeded in doing so in the past—a fantasy it will remain. Which brings us to examine the second half of the famed phrase that's become our standard economic operating instructions: all the work we're supposed to start doing and do hard.

EXHIBIT B: WORK HARD

If Americans do anything, it's work. We have less paid time off, shorter vacations, and more work hours than anyone else in the industrialized world. According to the International Labor Organization, "Americans work 137 more hours per year than Japanese workers, 260 more hours per year than British workers, and 499 more hours per year than French workers."[16]

At least 134 countries have laws mandating maximum hours of work per week. If you guessed the United States isn't one of them, you must work here! Add America to the club of one among industrialized nations for not having federally mandated sick days or annual leave. Ours is also the only country in the Americas without a national program that pays for parental leave. What Suriname, Paraguay, and Haiti have managed, we're still working out. If that's not enough, we also retire later than the residents of other nations; and with conservatives constantly devising new strategies to dismantle Social Security benefits, that elusive "entitlement" is likely to move even further out of our reach.

In short, if anyone needs to be told to work hard, it's certainly not us. To the contrary, some of today's most interesting and promising economic reforms barely getting mention would have Americans work less. Job sharing, thirty-five-hour workweeks, and longer vacations are suggestions our brightest economists offer to give more people the means to sustain themselves.

Americans' productivity has been, if anything, too great. In many cases, we've actually worked ourselves out of our jobs. As any management consultant can tell you, when you can accomplish all you need in fewer person-hours, you get to lay people off wholesale. You should try it; Mitt Romney assures us it's fun. The idea that Americans need to work harder when there's not enough work to go around would be comical if it weren't destroying people's lives.

As for those who *don't* have jobs—the vast and growing population we call "unemployed"—their problem emphatically isn't too much hammock time. It requires an incredible amount of work to hunt down, apply for, and piece together what's left of public assistance, such as food stamps and home heating discounts. Without a paycheck coming in, people without income also have to scour the landscape to find private charities to supplement public supports with big-ticket frills like vegetables or winter coats. The unemployed aren't lacking for things to do; what they're short on is earnings.

Admonishing the poor to work harder is so absurd it's almost comedic. Generally, those of us doing this urging have the great luxury of jobs we love. Jobs that are interesting, not physically demanding, and flexible enough to let us actually be ourselves. Who are we to ask waitresses and line drivers to work harder? Plus, as we've seen, directing people to work more simultaneously robs the employed of leisure and family time and ensures the rest an even longer struggle to return to a real paycheck.

Ultimately, as a mantra, "Work hard and play by the rules" says nothing about the economy we know we need to build or our role in it. In fact, this slogan remains entirely silent about the structural impediments to prosperity most of us face because of "the rules."

And while politicians in the center and on the left counter their opposition's arguments by trotting out this tired line, conservatives shoot verbal bullets. Those urging fiscal austerity voice their claims in the language of threats like "*apocalyptic pain*," as Senator Coburn did while also predicting the middle class will be "*destroyed*" by existing debt levels.[17] Compared to this kind of verbiage, our public rallying cry to return to an inequitable prerecession status quo verges on inaudible. And it's clearly not compelling. By making this statement, we turn ourselves into the kid running for class president on the "more homework, less recess" ticket. Vote for me!

I've pounced on what's admittedly only one sad little sentence in service of a much larger point: *words mean things, and the ones we pick matter*. The up-by-your-bootstraps and do-what-you're-told mantra makes easy sense to our fellow Americans, but it only reinforces a conservative worldview. It feeds and strengthens the very ideas Republican politicians need us to believe without questioning.

So too does the larger notion from which it emerges: that we must sacrifice ourselves for our GDP. This helps cement the idea that an all-knowing market left to its own devices will invariably set out unaided on the truest course for prosperity.

But why would those of us who know the economy requires external supervision, who care about distribution and not just acquisition, and who insist that environmental health matters keep implying the economy is best left to its own devices? Why would progressives, who disagree with the substance and assumptions behind conservative economic doctrine, reify these very same notions with the words that they pick?

OUR ECONOMIC PREDICAMENT, our debates about the need for fiscal discipline, and our difficulties making the case for reforming our financial institutions can all be tied strongly to the language we use to describe each one of these elements. Because we tolerated and even repeated tired tropes and meaningless metaphors, we mischaracterized the complex subject we sought to explain. And we're still at it. By continuing to employ language like "unhealthy," "suffering," and "recovery," we convey the message that the economy is something organic and self-regulating. Those of us on the left trying to change the system must then contradict ourselves by insisting, usually in the next breath, that the economy requires external control. Our message becomes muddled to the point of making no sense. This is the problem this book seeks to remedy.

During my career exploring the range of ways people understand complex political issues, I've seen one thing over and again: when we're using the wrong metaphor, we're sending the wrong message. When we frame our arguments with language that suggest that the economy is a deity, or even a lesser living thing, we make our favored economic policy solutions incoherent in the process. In fact, we pave the way for conservative arguments about slashing budgets and eliminating services as the one true path to economic success.

For those of us who reject the disproven notions that austerity and sacrifice are the lead solutions to our economic problems, we can get our message across. There are other, more accurate ways to understand the economy and our interaction with it. For those of us who never believed the rich paying less was the answer, there is still hope for change. By consciously shifting the ways we talk about the economy, clarifying our narrative for why we've landed in our current predicament, and characterizing what inequality is and what creates it, we can radically alter how we react to and thus make rules for the financial structures in our lives. In this book, I will show just how to do this.

Having studied how people come to judgments on issues from abortion to the economy and the environment to immigration, I've seen firsthand that too many of our progressive economic messages reinforce ideas directly at odds with our goals. But this doesn't need to be. We can stop implying what we don't mean. And when we do, we can begin to have a real, long overdue conversation about what we want and need as a society and how we should structure our economy to help guarantee these essentials.

DON'T BUY IT

CHAPTER 1

Once Upon Our Economy

The destiny of the world is determined less by the battles that are lost and won than by the stories it loves and believes in.
　—HAROLD GODDARD, *THE MEANING OF SHAKESPEARE*

One morning at a local restaurant, I struck up a conversation with a fellow diner who had sat down to breakfast with her picture-perfect young son. The problem, she lamented, was that after she had caved into his begging to come all the way there to order their legendary pancakes, he had taken two bites and refused to eat any more. The child cut in and said, "I'm only three!" In other words, were you really hoping for follow-through from a preschooler? What were you thinking, lady?

This sounds unfortunately close to the reasoning we have pushed folks to internalize about the economy. Current conditions may be troubling, if not outright unbearable. But what do we expect? It's the economy, for pete's sake—it'll do as it pleases! Now, please pass the syrup.

Worse yet, even those of us who outwardly profess just the opposite have transmitted at times the notion that Americans' hardships are of their own making. Or perhaps it's their free-loading neighbors who are to blame. Either way, the end result is to assume the only solution is belt-tightening, budget-slashing, total capitulation to the whims of Wall Street and big business.

For conservatives, ideologically opposed to regulation, taxes, public expenditure, and social programs in general, this is an ideal state of conceptual affairs. It helps keep the true causes of economic malfunction in the shadows. All the better to con-tinue and even double down on the failed "free-market" (a term subject to the interpretation of the proponent's choosing) ap-proach that got us into mess after mess in the first place.

The rest of us should run far away from this economic myth-making. If all of us who care about how *people* are fairing in our economy want to succeed in helping our fellow Amer-icans understand that the economy requires external super-vision, we must change what we imply about how it operates. While this change applies primarily to the activists, pundits, journalists, bloggers, economists, and politicians who most strongly influence our discourse on this topic, it matters just as much for those of us shouting at our conservative uncle across the Thanksgiving table.

A TALE WAITING TO BE TOLD

The 2008 housing market collapse caused untold harm to people at home and abroad. But it also opened up an opportunity, a giant fissure in the firmament of economic dogma. For decades, right-wing foot soldiers influenced by thinkers such as Milton Friedman and Thomas Sowell had trumpeted the theory that government governs best by getting out of the economy's way. They had dismantled New Deal protections, including the Glass-Steagall Act, which separated regular commercial banking from the speculative kind, and they eliminated underwriting standards for mortgages. (Granted, Democrats didn't put up too much of a fight and even helped along the way.) But then taking the form of a housing bubble, financial collapse, and recession, global-sized proof that deregulation was a disaster waltzed in.

Minted experts responsible for national monetary and fiscal policies operating under the notion that regulating financial markets stunts growth could suddenly be exposed as delusional at best and perhaps even merchants of deliberate misinformation. Former Fed chairman Alan Greenspan, a man so devoted to free-market orthodoxy that Milton Friedman and Ayn Rand would be proud to call him their love child, conceded his treasured theory didn't quite hold. As reported in the *New York Times*, "A humbled Mr. Greenspan admitted that he had *put too much faith in the self-correcting power of free markets.*"[1] Such are the perils of economy worship.

For those of us on the left, the message was clear. The events leading up to 2008 were a smoking gun aimed at the 401ks and home equity of ordinary Americans. People saw the whole thing go down and duly took out their smart phones to record it; a crime was committed, and almost all of us were the victims. This was a transformative moment. Democrats and progressives had their big chance not only to identify the current villain but also to go further: changing the conversation by introducing a new story about what the economy can and should be.

But we didn't.

From our greatest economic scholars to our labor union leaders to our elected officials, progressives offered our standard list of problems, all true, with business as usual. We published charts illustrating inequality and wage stagnation, featuring pictures of poverty, protests, and occupations. We got better at saying what, exactly, went wrong. But facts and well-deserved indignation alone weren't enough to mentally unseat what can generously be called a discredited ideology. As storyteller Jean Houston often says, "If you keep telling the same sad small story, you will keep living the same sad small life." The framework persisted, and the metaphors we used to convey these facts undercut any new narrative our numbers and charts displayed.

After eight long hard years of George W. Bush, triumphant at the arrival of president-elect Barack Obama, with a majority in Congress that included a filibuster-proof hold on the Senate, progressive advocates came to the crisis prepared with our standard full slate of policy demands. Fair wages for all, decent affordable health care, a secure retirement, and good public schools—the list is long, and most progressives can recite it verbatim. But conservatives never stop marketing their ideology to win over the public. They trotted back out the ever-popular critique that all of these goals, while certainly sweet, just wouldn't work given how the economy operates. Our problem, the nicer among them maintain, is we're simply naïve.

A joke basically every conservative I've met loves to recite tells of a man seeing newly born puppies at a pet store. He asks, what breed are they? An employee replies, "They're Democrats." A few weeks later, he stops in again and asks someone else, only to hear, "They're Republicans." The owner explains, "When they were first born, they were Democrats, but now they've opened their eyes."

And let's face it, there's some cause for the right to characterize the rest of us as well meaning but clearly delusional about the way the world works. We haven't spent all that much time demonstrating we get how things operate.

Laying out the progressive dilemma is fairly straightforward. We're pretty decent at saying what's wrong with the current economy; problem definition comes naturally to us. For example, too much wealth is concentrated in too few hands. Likewise, our goals are not only straightforward but also unquestionably popular among most Americans: affordable education and health care, living wages, secure retirement—in short, the promise of a middle-class life for all. The place we fall unforgivably silent is in providing proof that if you do X to the economy, we assure you Y will result. Because that's how the economy works, plain and simple. It's the *how* to get from here to there—from current calamity, inequality, and environmental destruction to stability, prosperity, and sustainability— where we say almost nothing at all. Or, to our detriment, cede economic explanations to an entirely conservative way of seeing the world.

Consider the most recent communication feat of right-wingers: turning the economic havoc that decades of their policies caused to their advantage. Hot on the heels of the economic unwinding launched in 2007 came a to-be-expected wave of public panic, pain, and confusion. Quite naturally, Americans wondered, what the hell happened? But lacking easily comprehended economic answers from us, many turned to the Fox News–fueled narrative of what had caused this mess. We had just won key elections, but conservatives seized the real political prize: the plot of our national economic storyline and with it the casting of heroes, victims, and villains.

Where life had decisively proven laissez-faire wasn't fair for the majority, Heritage, Hoover, and American Enterprise pundits managed to spin people back into seeing too much government at the root of the problem. The results were a wave of antispending, antitax, antistimulus rage and with it the 2010 midterm elections, which set state, local, and national governments decisively on a path to retrench conservative economic ideas and roll back progressive gains.

How could this have happened? Are Americans really so gullible, or more charitably, too busy looking for work, reading fine print, and scraping by for their health care to consider, think, and assess? Did we undergo some collective lobotomy between pulling the lever for Obama in 2008 and ushering in a Tea Party–packed House two years later? Those of us who work so diligently for progressive economic policies need to take stock of our unwitting contribution to this conceptual muddle.

We've already hit the tip of our economic messaging iceberg: those on the right and on the left alike have the tendency to refer to the economy as something natural, even divine. Too often, this cons audiences into believing that the way things are now, from serial bubbles to the financial collapse of recent years, is lamentable but largely out of our hands.

There's much we can do to change our language in order to tackle this problem, as we will soon see. Before we turn to this, however, let's outline the full size and nature of our communication challenge for the economy. Namely, our failure to recognize that in the debate for the policies we favor, progressives have no clear economic story, while our opponents push their free-market fable at full volume and at every instance.

The economic downturn opened up a window of opportunity for promoting an alternative economic vision. It's hard to imagine a better setup to introduce a new tale about the economy. But we didn't grab it.

As this chapter will show, we must understand the reasons for this failure to ensure we fix and don't repeat these mistakes. The fault lies partly in a pronounced shift in how we study economics overall, in what respected academics consider worth probing about this domain. This, in turn, becomes the basis for our unimpeachable truths about how the economy works and therefore how we should interact with it. Conveying how the economy functions is not optional; it's required for presenting a clear, believable storyline that supports why our proposed economic policies are the effective and right ones. Conservatives have mastered this narrative task. And until progressives can boast the same, we face the fundamental messaging dilemma of failure to explain and thus justify how the economy ought to be structured.

CREATING DEMAND FOR OUR BRAND

Marketing experts will tell you that the first task in selling a product is to create demand for it. If you want people to buy your new thing, you must first convince them it's something they shouldn't—nay, can't—live without. In recent history, we've seen countless new and unfamiliar gadgets become indispensable for large swaths of our population. Apple has arguably made its fortune convincing us we must have right now what we'd never even heard of yesterday.

Some of you will recall an era when portable phones were the size of squashes and only executives had them in their cars. Now, elementary school kids carry smart phones. Most of us can't imagine even leaving the house without mobile communication. Where we once lived blissfully unaware of cell phones, they've become—to many of us—another appendage.

In this case, the product we're long overdue to market is way less sexy than a new gadget. We need to generate public hunger for something entirely abstract: a storyline about what the economy can and should be.

Despite Democratic strategist James Carville's quip "It's the economy, stupid," getting Americans to listen to economic particulars has more often than not been a task made for masochists. In Carville's era and arguably decades before, economic ideas had to be boiled down to slogans that fit on a car bumper. Beyond the question of what's in my wallet and will there be more of it tomorrow, Americans simply aren't particularly drawn to knowing the details of what the economy is and how it works. Honestly, most of us choose to not even balance our checkbooks.

But in 2008 things really changed. Pew Research reported that in October of that year, 70 percent of Americans were following economic news. The previous peak in interest in this topic, during the downturn in early 1993, had won economic concerns an audience of 49 percent of media consumers.[2] As of 2008, the economy was *Challenger* disaster, O. J. trial, and Kardashian divorce all run together into one news-tastic package.

For decades progressive economists had been confined to academic obscurity with their discussions of inequality, the overreach of the financial sector, and other money-related concerns. Now they found themselves invited to be talking heads on primetime. Activists who had long sought to draw attention to the alphabet soup of mortgage-backed securities, collateralized debt obligations, and credit default swaps found a willing audience. Explain to me your acronyms; I suddenly care!

It was a golden opportunity for those of us trying to cement a new way of thinking about the economy. We had demand for our "product" dumped in our laps. At last, the public was convinced that the old ways of doing things weren't working. Americans were ready to question their assumptions, poised to consider an alternate view. An advertiser's dream, we finally had an audience wanting us to pitch our new good.

But instead of rejoicing and putting together a prototype for the public, we got bogged down in the specifics. We laid out generally unconnected explanations about who screwed up here and what went wrong there: it was the Fed and its monetary policy; blame the lax regulatory environment; look at the antiunion laws in many states that eroded real wages. But in reciting all of these truths, we were never really saying that the economy is this sort of thing and here's how it works. If you squeeze it, it will leak; if you stretch it, it will snap. And if you leave it absolutely alone, contrary to popular belief and conservative tall tale, it will harm the most vulnerable members of your society, in the process becoming so off-kilter that even those who have gated themselves off will feel the consequences.

We hoped that the facts would tell their own tale. Once people took a stark look at the numbers, they'd understand what we took for granted. This was no fluke; the system is indeed flawed. And, somehow, they'd absorb and feel confident about *our* solutions.

We gave great suggestions for regulations and new programs, and lots of them. Ideas for reforming the financial sector, tax proposals, health care legislation—hours of CSPAN tell the once-hopeful tale. But when we presented these policies disconnected from a compelling story, we forfeited our best chances to see them enacted.

IGNORING THE FOREST IN ORDER TO DISSECT THE BARK ON THE TREES

It's tempting to pin all the blame for this lack of clarity on the field of economics itself. These days, claims to credible theories or accurate predictions are about as believable from the Psychic Friends Network as from economists. At least the former offer some fun speculation about how many people you'll sleep with next month.

Exploration of how economies work has become remarkably circumscribed. A quick glance at economic course offerings at top-tier universities reveals a tendency to teach ever narrowly focused themes. Largely gone are the days of comparative economic systems and theories about communism versus capitalism. As economic researchers Roger Backhouse and Bradley Bateman contend, "We now have an economics profession that hardly ever discusses its fundamental subject, 'capitalism.'"[3]

By no longer examining capitalism itself, we've given up debating how it works best, what's flawed about it, and how to address these concerns. With the cold war behind us, and even the People's Republic of China communist in name only, domestic economists have decided to take American-style capitalism as a given. Now they're left just digging into the details.

What this approach offers in specificity it eliminates in vision. Dissecting economies with a microscope necessarily means being unable to perceive the whole. Backhouse and Bateman assert, "The questions [Occupy Wall Street] raise[s]—how do we deal with the local costs of global downturns? Is it fair that those who suffer the most from such downturns have their safety net cut, while those who generate the volatility are bailed out by the government?—are the same ones that a big-picture economic vision should address."[4]

In the absence of such examination, premises that we never challenge become and remain accepted truths. Too much is taken as given in our economic system. To start the list, I'd name these ideas: growth must be infinite, GDP is the valid measure of success, conservation takes a back seat, serious inequality is natural, and regulations are, at best, the lesser of evils.

Some, none, or all of these notions may hold merit. Perhaps, for example, the size of GDP does indicate something essential about a nation that no other type of figure could convey. But if we don't hold what are actually only assumptions up to scrutiny, it's impossible to credibly argue for or against any of these beliefs.

The "dismal science" seems to be growing increasingly so. In 2011, some students at Harvard University staged a walkout of their basic undergraduate economics course because it presented too much contested terrain as a given. The small group of students in the college's highest enrollment class claimed professorial bias in presenting an inequality-promoting conservative economic doctrine to the exclusion of other possible notions.[5]

When we don't ask for any grand explanation of how the economy can and should work, it's easy enough to fall into the trap of promoting one theoretical model as the only possibility. As biologist Stephen Jay Gould sagely instructed, "The most erroneous stories are those we think we know best—and therefore never scrutinize or question."[6] In this case, without a robust debate on what a well-functioning economy means, we will accept the standard of success we're most often handed.

What is that standard, and just what does it illustrate about the assumptions we take as given in our current system? If I smash all the windows of the cars parked on my street, GDP will go up because people will then spend money at repair shops and glass sellers to fix the damage. According to our current metrics, destroying someone else's car because I feel like it is counted as a net positive. (Bonus points if I serve prison time. This too generates a plus sign in the correct column.) Right now, the only serious attempt to put a chink in this paradigm comes from Bhutan; the country instituted an economic metric called "gross national happiness."

Progressives valiantly offer a litany of critiques of the status quo along with a vague sketch of economic Eden. And all of it may well be true and noble and necessary—I certainly think that it is. But if we say nothing about the economic mechanisms that would enable these changes, it's hard to believe we know how to do anything about anything.

Moreover, we don't just remain overtly silent about what I'm calling the how. We actually say quite a bit—most of it convoluted and at odds with our beliefs—by allowing our language to convey that the economy is self-governing and natural. What we transmit unconsciously about the economy generally reaffirms what conservatives want people to believe: government "intrusion" does more harm than good, and we just have to accept current economic hardship.

WHY THE *HOW* MATTERS

Conveying the mechanics of the economy is no esoteric exercise. If we fail to give a credible explanation for what makes the economy go haywire, we cannot make a compelling case for the policies we favor to set it right again.

Nobel Prize–winning economist Paul Krugman has offered an illustration of why if we're not explaining the how of our economy, our policies for it are dead on arrival. Krugman says, "I and others have watched, with amazement and horror, the emergence of a consensus in policy circles in favor of immediate fiscal austerity. . . . This conventional wisdom isn't based on either evidence or careful analysis. Instead, it rests on what we might charitably call sheer speculation, and less charitably call figments of the policy elite's imagination."[7] In fewer words, if we allow their fictitious story about how the economy works to hold sway, our opponents can justify policies that have proven disastrous time and again throughout the world.

Krugman even offers us a now widely repeated two-word phrase for our dominant economic mythology: confidence fairy. The notion here, championed by such economic giants as worst-president award-winner Herbert Hoover, is that slashing government spending will actually spur growth because businesses, observing our attention to deficit reduction, will feel great confidence and start spending. In arguing against slashing spending in a depression, Krugman remarks, "Pay no attention to those who invoke the confidence fairy, claiming that tough action on the budget will reassure businesses and consumers, leading them to spend more."[8] Never mind, as he notes, we've never seen evidence of this logic working. Its advocates pay no heed to the fact that our economy is 70 percent consumer spending, asserting instead that if we take money from those consumers, fairy dust (read: confidence) will magically make everything great.

But only the most self-interested elitists could possibly sub-scribe to such a ridiculous notion. Businesses must only pre-tend to buy this for the tax-cutting, regulation-slashing, operate-with-impunity mentality it helps promote. Surely, we can comfort ourselves with the notion that the general public has to know better. Right?

Unfortunately, this delusion appears to know no socioeco-nomic constraints. In fall 2011, Bloomberg asked a represen-tative sample of American adults what would be most likely to expand the U.S. economy and create jobs. Fifty-seven per-cent picked this answer: "Spending cuts and tax cuts will give business the confidence to hire." Contrast this with the 13 percent who said government spending ought to remain the same and the 23 percent who were in favor of an increase in spending as the best stimulant.[9]

Back in the reality-based world where you and I live, big business is doing very well, thank you for asking. Moody's re-ported that the 1,600-plus U.S.-based companies it rates sat comfortably on a record $1.2 trillion at the end of 2010, an 11 percent increase over the previous year.[10] One thing they're not doing with that big wad of cash? Giving you a job. But this pesky truth doesn't dislodge the idea that once businesses have enough money, they will do a better job spurring bigger, faster economic growth than the government could ever even contemplate. As the saying goes, "Don't confuse me with the facts; I've made my mind up already."

Die-hard believers in this give-to-the-rich approach will counter these stats with the claim that it's still too soon to judge. We just need to get *more* money to the wealthiest, and then they'll open the proverbial faucet. Get out your umbrellas—it will soon trickle down! The beauty of this thinking is that "soon," like tomorrow, never gets here and "enough" is a term subject to inflation.

The *Washington Post*'s Greg Sargent explains how Americans' tenacious attachment to the confidence fairy is an entirely predictable outcome of our lack of any accurate grasp of how the economy functions. Sargent says, "Dems have essentially lost the argument over whether government can create jobs, a problem that's partly of their own making, because they've essentially endorsed the conservative economic vision by agreeing to fight it out on the GOP's austerity/cut-cut-cut turf."[11]

We've all but conceded the way forward is to cut—that the economy is a thing you improve by choking off funds to it. Now we're just arguing over the details.

CONSERVATIVES COVER THE WHAT, HOW, AND WHY

The champions of the slash-and-destroy-in-order-to-grow model, a theory rivaled only by Creationism in its lack of reliance on evidence, may not have facts or historical precedent on their side, but they certainly have their how covered. In fact, they even offer us a bonus helping of why.

Part of this lies in their consistent use of very few underlying models, which all suggest the economy is a very specific entity that behaves in predictable ways. (We'll examine the details of this in the next chapter.) For now, suffice it to say on every level their language signals to us that the economy is something natural. Like any organic entity, it goes through expected cycles—we can think of this like waking and sleeping, reaping and sowing, summer and winter. To everything turn, turn, turn.

Conservatives, presenting a consistent message about what the economy is, set themselves up to convey clearly how it functions best. It requires external intervention only in cases of dire emergency; mostly, we're best left letting nature take its course. Expected fluctuations may be hard for us to handle, but we're no more able to regulate them than we could mandate it must be low tide at exactly 10 a.m. Pacific Time every day.

From this, it's easy to judge which policies are recommended and which will lead us down the sure path to destruction. Leaving well enough alone? Good. Altering "natural" signaling mechanisms like pricing? Horrible. This includes, of course, tampering with the pricing of labor by fiddling with minimum wage or maximum executive pay.

These conservative ideas are bolstered by the overt religious evocations and covert nature metaphors we've already seen. Not only do conservatives cover what the economy is and how it operates; their references to the economy as God-like explain what it's here to do.

The purpose is quite striking. The economy is here to reward the good and punish the bad. Competition is thus akin to commandments—by sending returns to the hardworking and depriving the lazy, free enterprise enforces the moral code we need our people to follow.

I can sum up the conservative view with a simple illustration:

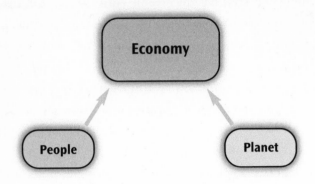

What conservatives make sure we imbibe—though rarely through overt directives—is the notion that people and nature exist primarily to serve the economy. Thus, the only valid measure of success is economic growth. If this comes at the expense of air quality, leisure time, life expectancy, or happiness, that's fine—all of these are secondary. Get out your togas; it's time once again to bow down before the Economy.

Granted, theirs is a compact and easily marketed worldview. But we're also doing lots of work for them. By our not offering up a clear alternative, theirs becomes the default understanding of the subject. And it gets worse. Much of the time we actually reinforce their framework through our lack of metaphor discipline, our reliance on essentially conservative tropes, and our inattention to the basic rules of effective communication.

Take, for example, our discourse on "government spending." Eric Liu and Nick Hanauer, in their book *The Gardens of Democracy*, aptly point out that *spend* means "use up"—

implying what's *spent* then is no longer with us. This feeds the fallacy about what government does with and to money. Paying out unemployment insurance or disbursing Medicaid funds is not the same as bespectacled bureaucrats lighting money on fire. It's government injecting resources into the economic system while also meeting critical human needs. These same funds then change hands again and again. They are not gone but rather have their efficacy multiplied through exchange.[12]

The problem progressives face is far clearer than the solution; the more complex and important question of fixing our economic discourse will be my topic for the remainder of the book. For the moment, it's critical to recognize the full extent of all we haven't even been trying to say. We need to convey what the economy is and, by extension, how it works best. Add to this a healthy dose of explaining what it's here to do. (Hint: make our lives better, not demand we do this for it.) Without a sense of the economy's purpose, a clear vision for the way things ought to work around here, it is impossible to make credible, popular arguments for proposals like increasing government spending especially as deficit mania looms large.

SIGNALING THE WAY TO OUR ECONOMIC DESTINATION

As Van Jones eloquently admonishes, Martin Luther King Jr. didn't get famous for saying, "I have a complaint." He also never said, "I have a policy proposal." Neither the memorable speeches of history nor the great slogans harp on the negative—and they certainly don't whine. They don't offer long lists, acronyms, or even much explanation.

If we want people to follow us, it makes sense to describe the place we'd like them to go. Even if that's the moon and there are no available rockets, it's important to name the destination if we're hoping to get people to go along for the ride.

As we've seen, for conservatives, the fundamentals are pretty straightforward. The point of the economy is to get bigger. Success means a larger GDP and a faster rate of growth. Failure is the opposite. The role of government is to promote increase, and this is best done by staying out of daily operations, incentivizing "good" behavior, and not rewarding undesirable actions. With this view as a touchstone, it's pretty easy to construct policies that accomplish these goals and perhaps easier still to create slogans for those policies.

So what's the progressive vision for the economy? What is the purpose of the economy in a just and well-governed world? What's the role of government in ensuring this vision comes to light? If the point of the economy isn't just to make more money, what is it?

There are powerful and vested interests preserving the status quo—and they have fully earned more than our ire. I'd say lots of them deserve some time behind bars. It makes sense that we're telling our audiences about their egregious sins and demanding they change. But this is simply not enough; we must also describe the world we'd like to see.

I am not so naïve to think, "If we build it, they will come." But if we don't build it, isn't it obvious they won't?

Nowhere is this lack of clear goal statement more striking than in our competing claims about our aims for handling differences in wealth and income. Both in surveying progressive writing and in talking with activists, I have found two distinct storylines about what we're seeking to achieve in this realm. These competing beliefs delineate the big economic inequality problem to be solved in roughly two ways.

1. Our job should be to eliminate extremes. Those with this view hold that massive wealth differences are problematic in and of themselves. They contribute to inflated and diminished self-worth at the affluent and impoverished ends of the wealth spectrum, respectively. They make society less cohesive. Not only is it unacceptable for people to have less than what allows for a healthy and fulfilling life; unrestrained riches are also problematic. Prominent authors such as economist Paul Krugman and journalist Barbara Ehrenreich offer us these summations of this orientation:

> If calling America a middle-class nation means anything, it means that we are a society in which most people live more or less the same kind of life.[13]

> Extreme wealth is also a social problem, and the superrich have become a burden on everyone else.[14]

The aims of this approach are well captured in the common refrain "Raise the floor and lower the ceiling." Unfortunately, it stands in contrast with the second, competing claim about the goal of addressing economic inequality.

2. The task before us is to increase economic mobility. Proponents of this notion hold that differences, even enormous ones, don't really matter as long as everyone has a fair shot at ending up in a different place than where they started. Believers in this claim tend to add that there must be minimal standards for health, safety, and well-being as well.

Note that this second point is only tangential to the overall thesis. Evidence attests it matters a lot to progressives that there be a "floor," but this notion is not inherent in this conceptual framework. If it were, proponents of it wouldn't need to make an overt case for it. Just as I don't need to tell you, "Come to my house, and I'll cook for you in my kitchen, where I cook." When something is a given, it doesn't require articulation.

Here are two succinct examples of mobility as the goal from political scientist Robert Putnam and policy researchers at the Economic Mobility Project, respectively:

> The fundamental bargain, the core of America, has always been that we can live with big gaps between rich and poor as long as there is also equality of opportunity.[15]

> Many Americans are even unconcerned about the historically high degree of economic inequality that exists in the United States today, because they believe that big gaps between the rich and the poor and, increasingly, between the rich and the middle class, are offset by a high degree of economic mobility.[16]

It's not my place, or my desire, to tell progressives which of these goals is the right one. But in the interest of full disclosure, I'll expose my own bias and say I've never found the mobility vision particularly persuasive. I believe extremes themselves—even in some imagined Horatio Alger utopia—are a problem. But this is the least of what, to me, is wrong with aiming our sights purely on increasing mobility.

If we were honest, we'd admit true mobility would have to occur in both directions—up and down the proverbial ladder. Otherwise, we would cease to have different income brackets. If everyone eventually made more, the top rungs would become unsustainably crowded.

For the son of the street sweeper to end up a CEO, the CEO's daughter must sometimes end up a street sweeper. This is the part of the mobility tale we take care not to mention. No one in the comfort of white privilege, as well as folks middle class or beyond of any race, would agree to a system where their children could end up in poverty. Consider the Rawlsian thought experiment of crafting a truly just society by having people imagine how they would distribute resources and even personal traits behind what he called "the veil of ignorance"—in other words, without knowing beforehand what lot they'd be cast.[17] Given how the world is currently structured, I hazard to assume the vast majority of Americans would not accept the gamble of leaving to fate where they end up. An all-bets-are-off unbiased global ladder would mean, for most of us, coming down many rungs.

Having variance in our views is not at all surprising. Many of us pride ourselves on a nuanced understanding of complex problems and a willingness to seek out and consider multiple solutions. This, in terms of crafting policy, is a major asset. In terms of communicating clearly, such multiplicity of views is a disaster.

In fact, you may see more commonalities than differences in these two "positions." But what matters is what the public sees. There's a lot of background noise in the world of politics. The messages that get heard provide a clear problem definition and solution. It's not obvious that folks on the left working on inequality are hoping to get us to the same place.

Again, my role is not to pick a goal, but rather to help us articulate well and clearly the one we prefer. Toward this end, I insist that in not having one, we're muddling our value proposition and making it hard for the public to understand what America stands to gain from implementing our policies. In short, having the public get behind us requires we have *a* dream—not a confusingly jumbled, somewhat related, at other times contradictory set of varying goals.

From my vantage point, our epic economic communication task is as follows. First, select and describe the economy we're seeking to create and sustain. Or if we truly can't get to this in the singular, be upfront that there's division among us about alternatives, like the two for addressing inequality mentioned for illustration above. And, second, convey to our audiences how the economy operates so that there's a clear line connecting where we are now to the place we want to head and with it, faith that progressive policymakers are the right folks to have in the driver's seat for the trip.

CHAPTER 2

What We'll Buy About the Economy

If you want to change the world, change the metaphor.
—JOSEPH CAMPBELL, *THE POWER OF MYTH*

We've now exposed a hard truth: progressives lack a coherent, compelling explanation for what the economy is, how it works, and what we ought to do to and about it. On the other side, conservatives win arguments and steer policy in their direction by telling a consistent tale not only about how the economy functions but also about its very purpose in our lives. We've talked a bit about the dangers of likening the economy to things natural and divine, but to really understand how we make sense of and eventually come to judgments about this particular abstraction, we need to go deeper. This requires delving into the metaphors we don't even notice we're using to make claims about the economy.

Of course, there are a host of practical roadblocks that prevent progressive policies for the economy from gaining traction. Politicians, scholars, and activists confront a formidable slate of barriers in their quest to reform our system of unfettered, undertaxed, and insufficiently regulated capitalism by implementing rules that would have us share prosperity among all. Through lobbyists and super-PACs, corporations influence and increasingly outright purchase political outcomes; notwithstanding the blip in excitement that was 2008, many citizens seem to care little and vote less; paid right-wing evangelists spread their messages on wholly owned and operated platforms such as Fox News, talk radio, and the *Wall Street Journal*. They've made themselves media that wear a veneer of legitimacy, on which they can present a single opinion as researched truth or dispense with these formalities to lie openly and often. And these are only the immediate obstacles that spring to my mind.

Important as they are, as you've probably noticed, this book addresses none of these. Instead, I focus on an equally critical one: communication. Namely, how to stop ourselves from presenting ideas that are at odds with our beliefs. In order to win any argument, what we say must reinforce the vision we seek to enact.

Granted, explaining the economy well is no small feat. It's justifiably hard to understand this topic. It even seems to stump Nobel Prize winners. Some of this is due to the nature of this complex and changing concept—derived partially from study of objective data, the rest dependent on the not-at-all-predictable winds of human desire and behavior. But some of the public's muddled thinking and assumptions are entirely of our own making—and continue to prove the unmaking of our arguments for change.

So let's temporarily set aside the nitty-gritty details of economics itself and look instead at something we have a chance at improving. By delving into how our brains make sense of complexity, we can unpack the unconscious comparisons or conceptual metaphors we most readily rely upon to wrestle with what this economy thing is. And armed with this knowledge, we can become more deliberate about what we say about the economy to ensure our words are actually what we mean.

Not all available ways of explaining the economy are created equal. Some have us default to believing it functions optimally when left to its own devices, while others profile the economy as a tool best used to meet our needs. Thus, understanding which simplifying models hurt our case for government involvement, environmental stewardship, and equitable prosperity and which trumpet the well-documented truth that the economy requires continual, smart, external supervision is no esoteric exercise. It's the fundamental first step to recognizing what inhibits Americans from believing in and rallying around our proposed policies to fix the economy, and it's the basis from which to craft our actual messages for those solutions.

CLEAR AS MUD

For much of the public, the economy makes about as much sense as tuning into Fox expecting to hear news. If you're like most adults and had little or no formal economic or financial education, cheer up; you're in good company. New research from the Economic Policy Institute (EPI) shows that even among members of Congress, including folks serving on the budget and appropriations committees, 80 percent have no formal training in economics either.[1] Those of us who did register for a class in the econ department likely remember, after seeing the intersecting lines of supply and demand curves, putting our heads down and hoping that no one would call on us for the rest of the semester.

Dartmouth economist Annamaria Lusardi, head of the Financial Literacy Center, studies the depths of our economic ignorance. She reports that fewer than half of adults can answer basic questions about inflation or interest rates—and we're not talking about making calculations, just simply knowing what these concepts are.[2]

Americans' myriad knowledge deficiencies aren't a secret—two-thirds of us couldn't name a single Supreme Court justice hot on the heels of the Sonia Sotomayor confirmation teleplay, one-quarter of U.S. teens guessed Christopher Columbus sailed here sometime after 1750, and forget about most of us finding Iraq on a map (six in ten eighteen- to twenty-four-year-olds can't master that task, according to National Geographic).[3]

But unlike all these examples, lack of economic or financial literacy has dire and proven personal consequences. People with less economic knowledge are more likely to have been foreclosed upon—even after figures are adjusted for such factors as income and education.[4] Those who don't understand the difference between an adjustable rate and a fixed mortgage tend to have the worst versions of the former.[5] A team of researchers from the Atlanta Fed, Columbia University, and the University of Geneva even found that many people buying homes could not accurately answer the question "How much will a $300 item cost at 50% off?"[6] These are the same people, of course, who are expected to calculate what variable interest rates will do to their monthly mortgage bill—or at least be on the hook to pay it.

What's worse, financial literacy is diminishing just as the expectations upon us to manage our own money grow. Roughly since 1980, American adults began to pay for some or all of our own health insurance, finance our own retirement, and borrow more for frivolous things like cancer treatments. Starting in this same period (and continuing today), the fine print on loans, mortgages, and other credit instruments turned microscopic. All this while even the mathletes among us remain hard-pressed to make sense of the exotic financial instruments Wall Street barons used to make themselves rich, crash the world economy, and engineer another fortune after getting bailed out for their blunders.

We could, of course, just shake our heads and toss this in with Americans' general lack of knowledge and understanding about . . . you name it, as evidenced above. But as we'll see, there's legitimate justification for this dangerous ignorance.

CAUTION! BRAINS AT WORK

Our modern, globalized, rapidly changing economy is hard to understand. But the language we use to describe it makes comprehension vastly harder. The standard ways we have of talking about economic concepts such as interest rates, inflation, and currency exchange all but guarantee no one outside the profession can make sense of them. Not only that, but given how infrequently economists voice accord on what action will yield what result, a fair number of them probably aren't quite sure what this economy thing is either. As George Bernard Shaw purportedly quipped, "If all economists were laid end to end, they would not reach a conclusion."

The economy is nothing concrete or tangible. You can't hold it in your hand, weigh it, or bounce it off the wall. Like we do with all abstractions, we make sense of the economy by comparing it to other, simpler things we more readily grasp. We compare intangibles to things that do have a readily recognized shape, weight, and form.

We may be tempted to call this process of simplification another sad side effect of our new 140-character-limit world. But this is no generational slide toward group ignorance. As cognitive scientists, psychologists, and linguists have revealed, it is an essential part of the ways our brains take in and process information. Unconscious comparison is the stuff of which reasoning and judgments are made.

We call one critical strain of this kind of thinking "conceptual metaphor," the unconscious and automatic process of comparing an abstract notion to another more concrete entity in order to better make sense of it. Decades of work from luminaries in linguistics such as George Lakoff, Mark Johnson, and Zoltan Kovesces demonstrate this reasoning at work.

As Lakoff and Johnson point out in *Metaphors We Live By*, people can make sense of something intangible like change in events by describing it as something experiential like forward motion.[7] We may get frustrated when our project doesn't *move forward* and we *hit a brick wall*; we may instead hope we can *get the ball rolling*, and we speak of *moving into a new career*.

Any time we produce nonliteral speech, which is literally any time, we're using conceptual metaphor. It's a habit so common, it's hard even to notice when our talk comes to rely upon metaphor. To offer another example, we're so used to the notion that *ideas are objects* that we routinely ask whether someone *grasped our point* or *it flew over his head*.

The situation gets interesting when we have multiple conceptual metaphors for the same notion. This indicates we are able to think about the same concept in a wide range of ways and thus influence what's "true" about it.

Powerful evidence now exists that *implying* different things about a topic—even while the overt assertions we make stay the same—can alter how our audiences perceive it. And, beyond this, can influence what they think can and ought to be done.

Stanford psychologists Paul Thibodeau and Lera Boroditsky found people much more likely to support stringent enforcement when crime was described to them as an opponent—a thing we must *fight back* or *beat*. In one experiment, 485 participants read short descriptions about crime rates in a fictional city and were then asked how they'd prefer to respond to the problem. Among them, 71 percent wanted more law enforcement if they read the description "Crime is a beast." This dropped to 54 percent for those who saw the words "Crime is a virus ravaging the city." Those who saw the second sentence, in which disease was the metaphorical basis for description, favored preventive programs as the means of addressing crime.[8]

Why did talk of disease trigger desire for prevention? Because this language led participants to consider unconsciously what they knew about illness. It's second nature to most of us that the best defense for the common cold is hand washing, that avoiding exposure to a contaminant can ensure we don't have to deal with various illnesses, that immunization, especially when done to an entire population, can make certain diseases all but disappear. In short, we are well aware of the efficacy of a preventive approach to diseases.

Amazingly, these associations can be compressed into a small space, with powerful consequences. The introduction of a different metaphorical comparison was the single sentence distinction between what the two groups of participants saw. Otherwise, everyone received identical statistics about rates of various crimes and changes to these over time. And, of course, subjects weren't consciously aware they'd been subject to this metaphorical priming. When they were asked what they based their decisions on, they insisted it was "the facts." Who doesn't want to believe himself a rational creature, swayed only by important things like evidence, research, and truth?

It isn't hard to see the persuasive possibilities this experiment suggests. Talk of crime being our opponent led to support for the traditionally conservative policy of greater enforcement and retribution. The other language, in which crime was likened to a contagion, bolstered a conventionally liberal approach of addressing the issue at its social roots.

Political operatives take note: while partisan leanings had some bearing on the outcome, the metaphor used to characterize crime was a stronger predictor of preference than party identification. Republicans were, not surprisingly, more likely to favor enforcement over social programs. But the language used to convey what crime "is" was far more effective than party line in nudging people to favor certain solutions. Perhaps there's still hope of getting through to most anyone.

A tiny wording change can mean the difference between switching people from one simplifying model to another—without having them know what's gone on. As litigators adept at leading their witnesses and advertisers can attest, persuasive ability improves greatly when listeners don't realize anyone is trying to convince them. Conversely, when we become aware of an attempt to make us see something a certain way, our conscious brain begins to weigh what we hear. Assertions like "Stricter enforcement reduces crime more effectively than preventive measures" are considered deliberately. They have us wonder, who is the messenger, and what is her evidence? Metaphorical shifts, in contrast, alter our assumptions about the topic set up for description without alerting us this is happening at all.

Crime in the aggregate is, of course, neither an opponent nor a virus. It isn't a "thing" in the strict sense of the word. But by likening it to one or the other of these concepts, we imply very powerful ideas about how crime operates and thus how best to deal with it. These embedded assumptions slip by undetected. And when we don't notice someone is feeding us critical judgments covertly, we can't consider whether they accord with our beliefs or contradict them.

Deliberately selected metaphor can be a persuasive communicator; it can help us privilege the set of ideas we'd love our audiences to understand. In fact, a whole slew of real-world experiments show just how much we can do by picking the metaphors we use to convey abstractions.

Prize-winning author and scholar of biology and neurology Robert Sapolsky offers us great examples. Among these, he reports on a study tracing attitudes toward immigration in which half the participants, as yet unaware of the real research topic, were made to read about health risks from airborne bacteria. Then these folks, along with the other half of respondents, were all given an article that likened the United States to a living organism. Researchers evoked this unconscious comparison by weaving in certain phrases, for example, calling population increase a "growth spurt." Participants who had read about bacteria first were far more likely to react negatively to questions about immigration than were their demographically similar peers who hadn't been "tainted" (pun intended) with talk of communicable disease.[9]

Clearly, there is profound power in metaphors and the assumptions they lead us to rely upon. However, we can harness the power of the unconscious only if we are keenly aware of what our words actually convey. To paraphrase conservative messaging guru Frank Luntz, we must pay attention not just to what we say but also to what people hear.[10] He should know. It was his messaging that in 1994 sold us the Contract with America, helping usher into Congress a Republican majority for the first time in forty years. Luntz also authored such doublespeak as "clear skies initiative" to market overturning air quality protections and "death tax" to make unpalatable to all something that applies only to 0.3 percent of taxpayers.[11]

Metaphors and simplifying models are the stuff of our everyday language; we draw upon them without realizing it to make ourselves understood. But right-wing messaging experts have perfected their use and abuse. Meanwhile, progressive politicians, pundits, and activists rarely pay heed to these issues. We continue to operate under the long-disproven notion that simply conveying well-researched truths will persuade; we cling to the notion that facts are our best friends and will set us free.

Undercutting our aims by citing the wrong underlying model is so common it might be the norm. Consider a national organization championing universal preschool and other great social programs preventing crime. Its name? Fight Crime Invest in Kids. While its supporters work diligently, with every breath and policy proposal, for programs they know will abate problems before they occur, they do so waving a banner that tells us to think about crime as our opponent. In doing this, they bias listeners toward thinking we need to get tough, not empathetic, with at-risk kids—just as they hope to convince the same audience that prevention costs less and works better.

Conceptual metaphors are so ubiquitous that they slip by unnoticed most of the time. Much of our speech is metaphorical; estimates have it that in every ten to twenty-five words, something nonliteral crops up.[12] (Take "crops up," for example!) We're transmitting a loud signal at a frequency we don't consciously perceive, even when we're the source of that sound. This is as true for what we say about the economy as it is for our communication about crime or immigration.

Since 2009, I have tracked and catalogued economic writing and speech from across the political spectrum. Considering diverse sources, from academics discussing specific Fed policies to "regular folks" bemoaning bailouts, from presidential speeches supporting a specific bill to radio show transcripts decrying the same legislation, I've seen that the menu of metaphors we employ to discuss the economy is vast.

But before we take a peek into what we're transmitting to folks about the economy, let's pause to consider what we'd *want* the public to get. A simplifying model is only as good as what we'd like it to highlight. Given the goal of enacting progressive reforms for our economy—higher tax rates for the wealthiest, increased revenue for long-term infrastructure improvements, and shoring up of our tattered safety net, among others—what would we have people understand and assume to be true about the economy?

DEFINING OUR BRAND: WHAT WE NEED TO CONVEY ABOUT THE ECONOMY

Every day, debates rage among scholars, politicians, and armchair pundits as to what individuals and governments should do, when, and for what duration to make the economy function better. Virtually every historic occurrence, every assumption, and every position can and does come into question in these disagreements.

Even defining what "better" means with regard to the economy is not obvious. Should we be trying to increase productivity, or is ameliorating our trade imbalance a better objective? Should we follow our usual course and spur yet more consumption, creating the "ownership society" we were told is our due? Or are environmental concerns about limited resources and limitless garbage more pressing than everyone having a home of his or her own? Consensus eludes us not only on whether to intervene but also, assuming we do, toward what end.

Below is my starting point for a wish list for the policy solutions we should convey to the public. I make no overtures toward objectivity—since it's my book, I get to pick. And, as I will be the first to admit, this list is far from exhaustive.

At a minimum, however, some elements aren't negotiable. Without these fundamentals in place, not much about a progressive economic policy agenda makes any sense. The truths progressives need to convey, but not necessarily say, about our economy include the following:

1. Government has a critical, continual role to play. We had an unfettered free market when we rode unicorns. And by this I mean never.

2. The system is global, not national. Capital holders move money from one place to the next. It's up to us to create the conditions to bring it to the United States. The wrong way to do this is making home the *cheapest* place to conduct business—eliminating corporate taxes, lowering wages, abolishing benefits, and doing away with environmental regulations. The right way is making our country the *best* place to produce—improving the intellectual capacity and skills of our workforce; ensuring public investment in what commerce requires, such as good transportation networks; and supporting vital

services like health care that make it possible for people to do great work.

3. Assessing costs and benefits in the short term makes sense only if we believe the apocalypse is immediately on the horizon. Spending money today on, for instance, great schools, roads, and health care pays off tomorrow in economic strength and growth, not to mention health and happiness. We don't save money by gutting social services; we merely kick our underlying problems down the road and make them larger in the process.

4. Environmental health and sustainability aren't an optional footnote. Person-made climate change, pollution, and water shortages, among the litany of environmental disasters, are crucial considerations in economic decisionmaking. There is no economy, or any you and me, without an inhabitable planet.

5. Vast inequality in income accumulation and overall wealth is both morally wrong and socially destructive; economic policy needs to address disparities.

This is not an ambitious list. Yet today we're hard-pressed to get the public to agree on and face these realities. Public opinion research demonstrates over and again that these seemingly obvious statements are deeply contentious and likely considered false in many Americans' minds.

Just after seeing an unregulated financial sector throw up all over our collective net worth like a kid at a frat party, 64 percent of Americans in a Gallup Poll listed "big government" as the largest menace to America. "Big business" was deemed the greatest threat by only 26 percent.[13] Another illustration, from a July 2011 Rasmussen survey of likely voters, showed 72 percent of them believing a free-market economy is best.[14] Admittedly, it's impossible to know what they were assuming this term means. But this is kind of my point—"free market" is such a good trailer people assume they'll love the whole movie. No need to read the reviews.

Even as extreme weather batters our people and property, ski resorts and surrounding towns go bankrupt, and ice fisherman can't solidly stand to get a line in the water, we see the environment as second, at best, to economic concerns. Presented the choice between environmental protection and economic growth, Americans in 2009 (and ever since), according to Gallup, waived their GDP pompons. This is the first time preferences followed this impossible order since Gallup began asking about how people would prioritize between economic growth and environmental protection in 1984.[15]

Granted, the false juxtaposition embedded in Gallup's question—that there is a choice to be made between economy and environment—is a perfect illustration of how poorly we understand both. Nevertheless, the thinking behind it—that there is an either/or between planet and profit—encapsulates one of many critical things Americans just don't get about either.

With the above-named requirements for how we conceive of the economy as a foundation, let's turn our focus onto the models used most frequently to talk about it. For each, we will consider how well or poorly it represents the facts we're trying to transmit and the story we're desperate to tell.

A MARKETPLACE OF METAPHORS

To recap, conservatives have mastered the practice of using the best models; it's hard to believe this is merely coincidental. Progressives need to play serious catch-up. While conservatives demonstrate admirable consistency, generating messages that suggest two or three models for explaining the economy, those on the left meander through many possible simplifications. It's no wonder our appeals for meaningful oversight often fail. We seem to not know what the economy *is*. Who would believe we know how to manage it?

These language missteps range from personifying the economy even as we claim it's not a sentient being, to relying upon frames that vilify taxation when we seek to increase revenues, to using phrases that make the financial crisis seem inevitable while we attempt to call for more oversight. Where conservatives continually employ language conveying the economy as independent natural force, we offer no such clarity of the opposite. We offer no clarity at all.

Only if our language conveyed an underlying notion of what the economy is could we then back up our case for how it ought to operate. Even when we have a strong sense of the policy solutions needed for a particular problem, we rarely set up our corollary explanation of the economy in the service of them. This is an egregious messaging error we don't need to be making.

Dead on Arrival: The Economy as a Body

"Suffering," "unhealthy," "no longer thriving." We've long described the economy in terms we should reserve for an elderly aunt. And when it's not health talk, we characterize our economy as if it were a wild teenager—always on the brink of major disaster, acting recklessly, without regard to consequences. Just who does this economy think he is?

Examples of likening the economy to something natural, most often a body, abound. From conservatives, we'd expect this approach—it accords with and indeed trumpets exactly what they want us to believe.

Nicole Gelinas, a scholar at the right-wing Manhattan Institute, remarks, "[People saving, spending, and investing don't] work so well when the economy is unhealthy." She goes on to unpack what unhealthy means: "That is, when the government is directing too much money into the housing market or into bad banks, hampering growth elsewhere."[16]

Gelinas's counterpart at the Heritage Foundation, Stephen Keen, questions, "Is President Obama's economic policy preventing the economy from recovering?"[17] This is far from a right-wing messaging habit—after all, Democrats named the stimulus bill the *Recovery* and Reinvestment Act. When haven't we found news accounts littered with references to economic "growth," the "health" of the economy, and debates about what the economy "needs"?

If the economy is a body, it's way out of shape. Perhaps the most vivid characterization of this type comes from David Mason, another Heritage pundit: "The financial sector is *flat on its back*. Government is working hard to *revive* it. A new dose of regulation and the uncertainty that it will cause is the last thing an *ailing* financial sector needs."[18]

This metaphor offers much poetic license. Note how Mason extends it to tell an entire story about where we are now and what we should avoid: "America's financial system has just suffered the equivalent of a *major heart attack*. In the long run, *lifestyle changes* are essential for the *patient's future health*. But the U.S. needs to get its financial sector *out of the emergency room* before insisting that it start *doing push-ups*."[19]

What are we really transmitting with language that ascribes characteristics normally applied to people onto the economy? Well, foremost, we suggest interference isn't welcome. When it comes to our bodies, we have agency and some measure of autonomy to act as we see fit. For most, our bodily functions don't require outside support. You seek out medical care in an emergency, but the daily business of digestion, circulation, respiration, and the like doesn't call for external assistance. Having someone tamper with your body's normal operations is not only annoying—it's also dangerous.

See, for example, Senator Rob Portman (R-OH), a man whose economic credentials include overseeing a 300 percent deficit increase as Bush Jr.'s director of the Office of Management and Budget: "Any tax increase would *hurt the fragile economy*."[20]

Once we're primed to understand the economy as most aptly akin to a body, periods of good and bad health are natural and therefore expected. Moreover, we know most conditions a body experiences go away unaided. So by applying body language, we're telling audiences to expect that periods of prosperity and recession are normal and emphatically don't require government intervention; most fluctuations to the economy will adjust on their own. In times of extreme crisis, the economy *may* require outside interference, but even so, this should be as minimally invasive and short-lived as possible. Back off politicians; first do no harm!

With this model firmly in place, it makes perfect sense to argue, as Cato Institute's director of tax policy Chris Edwards does, "Policy-makers need to decide whether they want to continue mortgaging the future or letting the economy adjust and return to growth by itself, as it has always done in the past."[21]

This language helps promote the view that when it comes to the economy, government is best that governs least. If the economy is understood as a body, restrictions (i.e., regulations) on it are unnecessary, unfair, and ill advised. Just as Yaron Brook, president of the Ayn Rand Institute, told Glenn Beck on Fox, "We're taxing, regulating *to death* American industry, American free markets, American capitalism, and there are not going to be jobs anywhere."[22]

Drowning Our Arguments: The Economy as Weather and Water

When it's not a body, the economy is spoken about as some other natural element: the weather, the tides, the life force itself. We speak, for example, of "weathering economic storms."

Like a liquid, money moves freely. Like the tides of an economic ocean, money rushes in and out. As an editorial for *The Week* tells us, "Prudent regulation helps contain the harmful spillovers of productive activity."[23]

In discussion of the economy, we hear frequent mention of "flow." Here's an example from another Heritage pundit, Karen Campbell: "In a global economy, investments will flow to the areas where they can earn the highest returns."[24] Isn't it amazing how money can pick its own destination? This construction mashes together the metaphor of money as liquid with a dose of personification. In the process, money or capital becomes construed as in control—it knows what it wants and makes things happen.

The implications of this model amount to nothing less than a conservative wet dream. Heritage, Cato, Fox News, and Republican politicians love peddling it because in so doing, they elegantly transmit everything they need us to believe—conditions are natural, external control is either impossible or harmful, and outcomes are as God intended. You know who regulates the ocean? The moon.

Considering how potent (not to mention absurd) this metaphor is, you'd expect progressives and even centrist Democrats to avoid it at all costs. Those of us who know such conclusions are crazy would never use language that suggests economic regulation makes as much sense as mandating when it will be high tide, right? Actually, folks on the left embrace this language.

New York Times columnist and *Conscience of a Liberal* author, Paul Krugman, is an especially big fan of this metaphor. He uses it here to describe the onset of the financial crisis: "The result was a world *awash* in cheap money, looking for somewhere to go."[25] And he continues with it to characterize outcomes for individuals when things went wrong: "[people whose] assets have *evaporated* but whose debts remain all too real."[26] This sadly reinforces the idea that things just happen— no one does or decides anything, so no one is to blame. The retirement money you've been saving for decades? Practice your crawl stroke; it went out with the tide.

Krugman is in good company. EPI, a proudly progressive think tank, advises that when government spends money, "it creates beneficial *ripples* through the entire economy."[27]

True enough, but why use this metaphor to transmit this information?

Again, just like body or weather models, water talk suggests the economy is a natural system, which therefore self-regulates. As an unfortunate side effect, inequality becomes a nonissue. If resources move freely through the economy, there can be no "right" or "wrong" place for them to be—they'll just head where nature intends them to be.

This model profiling economic activity as like liquid moving through a system forms the conceptual basis for the discredited "trickle-down" theory we love to hate. It's wholly at odds with our most basic assumptions about government intervention as necessary and beneficial. As long as the economy is understood as a natural and self-regulating system, it will be hard to make the case for policies directed at changing where money "flows."

Who's the Boss?

It's not just via metaphor that we fall into these messaging traps. Our willingness to accept that the economy itself ought to be our chief concern makes it easier to hold us in thrall to its seemingly inexplicable whims and constant needs. It's just so easy to irk the economy; we must not dare think about ourselves.

Say it with me: "The economy is nothing more than the sum of our collective endeavors." If we prick it, it does not bleed. For those of us who believe the economy (whatever that means) requires external control and supervision, referencing it in the language of people, weather, and water undercuts our ability to make this truth known. For those of us who see an all-too-unfettered market as a sure path to calamity, speaking about the economy as a freewheeling agent, capable of action and even foresight, makes no sense.

Yet we routinely say, "The unemployment rate is rising" and "The dollar is falling." As if these simply come to pass. Like sands through the hourglass, so are the economic days of our lives.

This passive language obscures the choices behind these outcomes. The decision, for example, to lay off public sector workers and add them to the ranks of the jobless "drives up"—you guessed it—that darn unemployment rate. The choice to extend tax cuts for our wealthiest and twiddle our thumbs instead of closing corporate tax loopholes made municipalities and even some states go entirely bankrupt for want of the revenues these sources can and should supply.

Awarding the economy agency also lets off the hook the folks George W. Bush might have called "the deciders"—if he were willing to share this title. The policy whims of wealthy elites, made possible through national, state, and local government officials, are no natural disaster. When these people cut services, starve social programs of funds, and neglect infrastructure, they are deliberately destroying our nation. Letting the economy's movements be described as natural or self-willed prevents us from holding people in power accountable.

Yet the left can't seem to resist continually employing language that puts the economy and not people in the subject position—phrases that suggest the economy manages best on its own. Community organizer turned media personality Sally Kohn charged that Wall Street "tried to gain a profit as our national economy *lost its shirt*."[28] And once again from EPI, "The U.S. economy is not *suffering* alone."[29]

In fairness, it's understandable why progressives employ language that evokes these unhelpful notions. These are, after all, unconscious comparisons, and as speakers of a shared language community, we're hard-pressed to go against the prevailing, undetectable tide of communication on a popular topic.

But that doesn't make it any less frustrating. Folks who believe the economy isn't an independent entity must stop embracing language that suggests it is. Doing so only advances the ideas of those on the right.

Wrong Side of Rhetoric: The Economy as a Moral Enforcer

Not all simplifications need to be metaphorical. In a CNN segment that asked "real people" to propose economic solutions, Cliff Hilton, a Texas restaurant owner and father of two, crafted an allegory for a beloved right-wing position:

> If I consider a plot of land, prepare the land (remove rocks, trees, weeds), plow the rows, plant the seeds, and pray to God for sunshine and rain, am I required to give the [harvest] to someone who never put their hands to help nor their money and health at risk for failure or success? Don't dilute my expectation. If I fail, I fail alone. No one wants to help pay for my failure. If I succeed, you should not want to take my money and give it to one who has failed.[30]

Hilton's analogy hammers home a shamelessly reactionary vision of how America should work. In case you've forgotten the rules of preschool, a shorter version of his story would read, "Mine, mine, mine."

Lost completely on Hilton, and indeed all the Tea Partying people espousing this "government hands off my money" mentality, is that, though he may have benefited from his own labors, he didn't create the sun or the rain. Yet not a single plant in his tale could have been harvested without either. The "public goods" in the real economy story—the roads we require to transport ourselves, the basic schooling we need to train us for the workplace, the health care we need to keep us well enough to work—are created for and thus by everyone.

The message of how the economy operates here is not implied—it's direct. We see it echoed in statements like this one from John McCain (R-AZ): "Conservatives do have solutions, including letting bankruptcy and the free market strengthen business, not punishing success through taxation and building our nation's debt to prop up the status quo."[31]

In this view, taxation is not the collective pooling of resources to pay for what the group needs. It's a form of punishment—and makes little sense if you believe the purpose of the economy is to reward and encourage "good" behavior while disincentivizing and curbing "bad" behavior.

Hoover Institution scholars Henry Olsen and John Flugstad, in the midst of a rant about the evils of "entitlements," hammer home this mentality:

> The first principle, largely traditionalist in nature, is that when government programs are established, their structure and administration should *support and enhance traditional virtues* (and certainly programs should never undermine such

virtues). In practice, this means ensuring that government programs sustain and enhance attachment to the work force, encourage the *cultivation of traditional moral virtues like self-reliance and ingenuity*, and support rather than weaken the appeal of *the traditional family*."[32]

This moral slant on all things economic can be found almost everywhere in contemporary discourse. Libertarian Alan Reynolds lamented on National Public Radio about the nefarious effects of caring about people's ability to live, saying, "When the government takes money from those who earn it and gives it to those who didn't, that discourages both of them from earning more."[33]

Not only are unearned rewards deleterious for individuals; they also make corporations behave badly as well. So notes conservative darling Matthew Continetti: "Direct cash assistance—the bailout—*fosters a culture of dependence and entitlement. It does nothing to discourage irresponsible corporate behavior*."[34] But this isn't all that surprising a connection. As the Supreme Court reminded us in its decision expanding campaign contributions by likening these to free speech, *Citizens United*, corporations are people.

According to this framework, the economy has a very important job to do above and beyond producing and distributing goods and services. The economy is a source of moral order. It helps establish and police proper behavior, rewarding those who do right and forcing those who don't to get with the program.

Our most conservative lawmakers now keep themselves occupied trying to turn this moral code into actual policy. For instance, as a part of the deliberations over extending unemployment benefits through the end of 2012, Republican lawmakers sought unsuccessfully to mandate drug testing for anyone soliciting unemployment insurance.[35]

This wasn't a onetime excursion into moralizing by other means. As of 2011, conservative legislators in two-thirds of states are seeking to add drug screening to the gauntlet of hurdles for receiving welfare payments. In Mississippi this would include checking for nicotine. Under these plans, unemployed and welfare-eligible individuals pony up for the cost of the test and then government is on the hook to reimburse them if their results come out negative. Florida, for example, where a law to test welfare seekers was in effect for roughly five months until a federal judge blocked it, shelled out $1,140 for thirty-eight negative tests against a savings of $240 in benefits for the two individuals with positive results. (And this doesn't include what the state had to pay to lose at defending the policy in court on the first round and continues to spend in appealing the ruling.)[36] But I guess self-avowed deficit hawks don't seem to mind racking up the costs for this expensive endeavor.

Again, it doesn't seem to matter to these representatives that previous attempts to do this have been thrown out in court or that credible research shows drug use is no more common among public assistance recipients than anyone else in our country.[37] When it comes to promoting desirable habits and punishing the people who get out of line, money and constitutional rights prohibiting unreasonable search are suddenly no obstacles.

Nowhere is this role of the economy as an enforcer of a highly subjective moral code more astonishing than in the very existence of self-identified proponents of small government who find themselves unwittingly suckling at the poison teat of public assistance. Lucky for them, the ability to believe two completely contradictory ideas at once is another wonder of the human brain. When that proves too difficult, there's our even more highly evolved technique of sticking our fingers into our ears and yelling more loudly than what we don't want to hear.

We see time and again people resorting to a standard method of reconciling what they don't believe in (government handouts) with what they receive (government handouts). Take, for example, the infamous Tea Party rally sign that reads "Get government hands off my Medicare." Further, a 2008 Cornell Survey Research poll of representative Americans had 57 percent of the 1,800 respondents claiming to have never received government aid. But 94 percent of these same people then recalled having accepted either Social Security benefits, federal students loans, unemployment insurance, or some other form of—say it with me—government money. The average participant had benfitted from four of the forms of assistance. These contradictions demonstrate just how Americans, in the face of lived experience, hold proudly onto a view of themselves as self-made, with the corollary idea that public benefits foster a culture of lazy dependence. Is it any coincidence that a nearly identical proportion—56 percent of respondents in a different poll—said they wanted smaller government and fewer services?[38] Only very bad people need and accept government handouts; the morally upright take care of themselves.

It's quite easy to have your cake and bitch about it too. Throw in contempt for other eaters, sanctimonious diatribes about the calorie and fat content of dessert, and attempts to destroy the baker and you've pretty much summed up the Tea Party. It's sad, really: cake goes so nicely with tea.

But for those who don't allow themselves the comfort of self-deception, there is real pain in taking the life-saving government aid that they've been taught to see as deeply wrong. In a widely cited *New York Times* article, Binyamin Appelbaum and Robert Gebeloff reported on this phenomenon: "When pressed to choose between paying more and taking less, many people interviewed here hemmed and hawed and said they could not decide. Some were reduced to tears." For many of the people with whom Appelbaum and Gebeloff spoke, public money, most notably subsidized medical care, is a matter of literal life and death. Nevertheless, they seek to diminish or even demolish the programs that sustain them.[39]

For some, unconscious acceptance of the economy as a moral enforcer enters into the potent realm of religious belief. The free market becomes nothing short of a doctrine. Over the past fifty years, adherents of the so-called prosperity gospel have preached that material wealth is a sign of favor from God. High-wattage pastors like Joel Osteen, Jimmy Swaggart, and Jim Bakker helped merge the pull-yourself-up-by-your-bootstraps just-so fable with the language of faith. The New Testament may declare it easier for a camel to go through the eye of a needle than for a rich man to enter the kingdom of heaven, but these modern-day money ministers teach parishioners that God's blessings come with bonuses and stock options. *South Park's* parody of economic idol worship begins to look like reality television.

The ramifications of this model are profoundly negative for progressives. Thinking about the economy as a tool for enforcing morality makes any government intervention hard to stomach, especially programs that give special help to those who've proven themselves least worthy: the poor. It also makes justification for *not* helping these losers much easier to market.

Enter, stage right, the rehash of the old argument that poor people's problems are their own lack of morals. Libertarian political scientist and author Charles Murray in his recent book *Coming Apart* has once again trotted out the theory that, no matter how unequal our society, the real hurdle people face stems from their own lack of values. (Fortunately, unlike in his previous, much-reviled volume *The Bell Curve*, at least this time he confines himself to lecturing only about and to white people.) Murray points to the link between economic status and people not getting or staying married, plus out-of-wedlock birth.[40] And here we thought people were poor because they didn't have money!

People who privilege this model may care about the benefits we catalog in support of our policy solutions, such as economic growth, an end to recession, and lower crime rates. But they care as much or more that the economy enforces what they consider good habits (thrift, hard work, initiative, marriage) and punishes bad ones.

Making the case that your proposed policy will boost the economy itself or save money in the long run to someone who reasons from this model is like trying to persuade an Orthodox Jew that a particular restaurant makes the best ham and cheese sandwich. Good luck with that. Increasing the GDP, improving productivity, restoring infrastructure, or creating whatever benefit you name doesn't matter if it interferes with the ability to shape behavior through economic incentives.

Of course, "right" and "wrong" are in the eye of the beholder. For people like me, the correct and moral role of the economy is maximizing social good, protecting the natural environment, and providing to all such essentials as a living wage, secure retirement, health care, and leisure time.

Progressive pastor Jim Wallis, for illustration, poignantly entreats lawmakers to see the economy through a moral prism. In arguing for helping the poor at home in lieu of bombing them abroad, Wallis sermonizes, "Our nation needs the affirmation that *budgets are moral documents*, but also that leaders are willing to commit to a vision of recovering some of our nation's greatness. We must hear the words of Dr. Martin Luther King Jr. in 1967, and think about the realities and ramifications of the war in Iraq: 'A nation that continues year after year to spend more money on military defense than on programs of social uplift is *approaching spiritual death*.'"[41] As the budget is most assuredly the framework through which we establish and make good on our beliefs about what matters to us in society, his argument is certainly one worth heeding.

Others on the left side of the political spectrum, such as former secretary of labor Robert Reich, urge that transparency plus our inherent moral framework must undergird our consumption decisions:

If the market mechanism were so transparent that we could not avoid *knowing the moral effects of our buying decisions*, presumably we would then have to choose either to sacrifice some material comforts for the sake of our ideals or to sacrifice the ideals in order to have the comforts. That would be

a true test. Absent such transparency, we don't need to sacrifice either. We can get the great deals and simultaneously
retain our moral scruples without breaking a sweat. The market does not corrode our character. Rather, in these two ways,
it enables us to shield ourselves from any true test of our
character. It thereby allows us to retain our moral ideals even
when our market choices generate outcomes that would otherwise violate them.[42]

Having consumers pay heed to working conditions, pollution, and health hazards endemic to many productive endeavors could make those activities less profitable and eventually
more rare. If people stop buying pesticide-coated strawberries
to protect their own health or out of concern for the pickers,
we may one day cease to see these particular fruits in our gro-
cery stores.

Positive applications notwithstanding, the well-entrenched
model of the economy as a moral system serves the assumption that the rich are well-deserved winners and provides great
reasons to screw the rest of us. The standard usage of this language does not lend itself to a progressive view. It not only reinforces the idea that government should stay out of social
spending; it also loudly demands this. The economy's function
is to affect behavior; it should encourage people to work hard,
earn lots, and look only to themselves to meet needs. Actually,
"should" is too weak here. The better descriptor is must.

This is, at its core, a Darwinist view of the economy: winners are those who capture available resources, become financially fruitful, and multiply. The system weeds out those who

can't. Thus, this fits in perfectly with notions of the economy as a natural entity. Nature punishes or enriches those who adapt best to her whims. This is neither good nor bad; it's simply the way the world works. Stop whining about it.

On the Right Track: The Economy as an Object in Motion

In stark contrast to naturalistic and moral language, there's a highly recommendable metaphor that refreshingly suggests the economy is a human-made object. Simply put, to activate this notion, we compare the economy to an object that's in motion.

Often the more specific object of choice is a vehicle, for which the speed, direction, and duration of motion naturally stand out as critical concerns. We can argue, for example, about the need to "rev up our economic engine." Likewise, we can debate whether the economy is "on the right or wrong track" or "stuck in a rut." Progressive economists like James Galbraith and Joseph Stiglitz have communicated in this framework by putting forth ideas about what should "drive" our economy.

Justifications for the stimulus relied, not surprisingly, upon our ability to understand the economy as an object in motion. Like this one from left-leaning Washington think tank the Center for American Progress: "An economy suffering from lack of demand needs a jump-start."[43] So too do attempts to explain what we've experienced over the last few years. As *New York Times* economics columnist David Leonhardt puts it, "The economy has been lurching from one crisis to the next."[44]

At the end of 2011, promoting his new jobs bill, President Obama admonished, "Now is not the time to slam the brakes on the recovery. Right now, it's time to step on the gas."[45] Similarly, in his attempts to advocate for fellow Democrats in the 2010 midterm election, Obama often trotted out lines about voting for Republicans and not Democrats was a surefire way to send our economy into R and out of D. By this he meant, of course, reverse and drive.

This model is also at work whenever concern over the economy is expressed in terms of its movement, relative speed, and direction. Two journalists note, "The economy remains deep in a recession."[46] In other words, mired in a ditch and no longer advancing. Along these lines, we can describe economic problems through references to lack of motion: "The economy, when left to itself has the potential to get far out of balance, and even get stuck in dead-end traps."[47]

The metaphor is supple enough to work in the other direction too—the economy or its indicators can be moving too fast in the wrong direction. In 2008, when Hillary Rodham Clinton was running against the man who became her boss, her campaign produced an ad featuring a skydiver, as a dramatic voiceover declared, "Our economy could be heading into *free fall*." It's likewise commonplace to hear about "accelerating job losses." Or in a rare show of conservatives going off their preferred nature metaphors, Tea Party–backed candidate Scott Martin said, "I can no longer sit idly by and watch as the American economy continues its *agonizing descent*."[48]

There are seemingly endless ways to describe the economy in the language of motion. Economics routinely uses terminology from physics like friction, stability, equilibrium, and elasticity—descriptors of movement through space. We can also say the economy "has fallen off a cliff" or needs to get on the "right path" or, in other words, on a "new course."

While many of these kinds of references suggest cars, others liken the economy to a train ("get back on track"), a ship ("sinking"), a balloon ("lifting," "Tax hikes weigh down the economy"), and a ball ("bounced back," "Stocks today rebounded"). And, as noted above, we constantly see mentions of the path on which the economy moves and whether it's the right one ("new avenues of economic advance") or wrong one ("The downward spiral will continue").[49]

Progressives have many reasons to use the language of such a model. First, an object in motion generically, and a vehicle more specifically, is almost always person-made. Our immediate association here, especially given the actual language we find, is of a complex thing people build to do their bidding.

Second, and equally critically, a vehicle actually requires an external operator. It absolutely does not run itself, nor would we want it to do so. A driverless vehicle is a safety hazard. Likewise, a free and unfettered economy will "crash," just as bad government driving led it to do at the start of the Great Depression. This model offers us the chance to argue that the government can "steer" the economy or create "rules of the road."

In fact, Obama employed just such a metaphor in an Osawatomie, Kansas, speech intended to reboot his reelection campaign and promote a more populist economic program. On December 6, 2011, a date deliberately chosen as the anniversary of similar words from one of his presidential predecessors, Obama said, "Roosevelt also knew that the free market has never been a free license to take whatever you want from who-ever you can. It only works when there are *rules of the road* to ensure that competition is fair, open, and honest."[50]

A disclaimer: this metaphor is far from foolproof. While it provides a space for government activity, unlike the previous simplification we saw, it doesn't automatically include this role. When we read, for example, "The economy continues to tank,"[51] both the reason for this undesirable movement and the recommended solution to it are left unspecified. This stems from another, widespread problem we've touched upon and will revisit: failure to name villains, heroes, and victims. Establishing the sources of harm as well as the legitimacy and desirability of government involvement is an important foun-dation for many of our policy prescriptions. Object-in-motion language is necessary but not sufficient for this task.

Just to complicate things, the free market is also refer-enced as an object in motion (sometimes a person), but one that doesn't require or indeed even offer a role for an external controller. The critical differences is that the free market is talked about as much more like an atom, whereas the econ-omy overall is a complex, deliberately built entity. This is what makes it possible to make a strong case for having someone at the wheel.

There remains much to debate about who should drive this economic train and how. For example, "Richard Shelby, top Republican on the banking committee, warns Cassandra-like that Obama's budget will put the country on 'the fast road to financial destruction.'"[52] But what's critical here is that this model at least allows progressives an avenue to make their case. In contrast, the organic language of health, weather, and water makes that all but impossible.

Describing the economy as an object in motion even allows for interesting and effective arguments for addressing inequality. It is not difficult to extend this conceptual metaphor by talking about needing to let everyone on board so that we all travel together into the future. When we convey that wealth and income inequality results from leaving folks off the vehicle that propels society forward, it becomes much harder to think of the poor as lazy, unmotivated, and undeserving of financial reward. Addressing equality no longer seems like offering a handout; it's a matter of simply giving everyone a seat on the bus.

Getting There from Here: The Economy as a Means to Facilitate a Journey

Conservatives have won elections and diverted policy to their ends by switch-hitting between two important conceptual models: the economy as a natural entity and the economy as a moral enforcer. The former tells audiences *what* the economy is—what it needs and therefore how best to handle it. In case it's not obvious, the answer is, most of the time, just leave it alone. The latter makes the unconscious case for conservative policies in another way. It tells us *why* the economy exists—what job it does in our society.

We've now explored the best potential progressive take on what the economy is. The why is not nearly so obvious. Just when I despaired of finding a corollary on our side for conveying the purpose of the economy, however, I conducted anonymous one-on-one interviews with some of our greatest pro-gressive economic thinkers. Although it rarely comes out in our writing, it turns out we too have a nonmetaphorical model for the economy. We explain ourselves by signaling that the economy is a means to facilitate journeys. And I believe it's our ticket to explaining the experiences (negative and positive) of the individual in the economy as well as selling our vision of how things can and should work.

When we think about vehicles, salient considerations in-clude the quality, direction, and speed of movement. Does your car have proper shocks to absorb any bumps? Is the road scenic and well paved or ugly and potholed? Are there giant obstructions or traffic jams making it impossible to go on your way?

The vehicle model allows us to vividly describe the econ-omy itself. But sometimes we need to look inside and under-stand the experience of the people—the vehicle's passengers. Especially when we're seeking to make claims about the ob-stacles to economic prosperity, like receiving less pay for an honest day's work than your colleagues or seeing your house's value plummet while bankers make millions from bad mort-gages. It isn't so different from seeing someone cut across five lanes of proverbial traffic by exploiting loopholes and dodging regulations, because he considers himself so special the rules don't apply.

For this critical task we can apply one of the most common and evocative conceptual metaphors in our language: life as a journey. This gives us everyday expressions like *stuck in rut* or *at a crossroads*. Our relationships or careers can be *going nowhere* or *moving along*. And then there are those *carrying lots of baggage*, which makes it much harder to continue on their way.

The following examples, paraphrased from my conversations with various economic thinkers, may seem quite similar to those we saw above in describing the economy as an object in motion, but shot from a new angle. Now we zoom in from seeing the whole system to focus on the people within the economy:

> Well, because if you don't have [government,] then you have individuals *pulling each other in different directions*, and this leads to *gridlock*.

> [Government spending] gives *rein* for individual initiative and innovation.

As we'd talk about letting out the reins on horses to spur them along, this word describes a freedom of motion. But in this case, it's for people's *ideas*. Another respondent used it to characterize curtailing movement by saying, "When people are fearful for the future, they tend to rein in on their demand for goods."

This turn from the social—the economy overall—to the experience of individuals comes up especially when talk turns to inequality. Because relative deprivation matters so much for the people experiencing it, this much more personal model can be a powerful one to vividly convey current problems.

The name of one of our national programs for equalizing outcomes, Head Start, speaks to this model's power. Several folks with whom I spoke used related language:

> And I think every child in this country and other countries should have the same opportunity [to ensure] we're all at the same *starting point* in life really.

> Some people are gonna *come out ahead* of other people. But at the starting gate, it ought to be equal.

> There is always the problem of luck . . . and of course that's why we have social policies, . . . You *find yourself in the wrong place* at the wrong time, [and] then you have things like unemployment insurance, workman's compensation, or social security disability—all these things to kind of help you out.

Beyond providing apt language for the problem of inequality, the notion that the economy is or ought to be a means to facilitate our journey in life is a powerful and deeply American ideal. The "pursuit of happiness" enshrined in our Declaration of Independence is actually about unfettered motion. It relies upon the life-as-journey metaphor so common it's perilously close to becoming cliché.

A couple of interviewees evoked this idea in describing an ideal economy:

> You have ideal chances *to wind up where you want to be*. . . .
> [When there] is something you want to do, you choose to do,

you pursue, and you're able to realize it with reasonable expectations.

[Profit is] to be used as a *mechanism to push people*, maybe sometimes against their better judgments, to make the world a better place.

The metaphor of the economy as a vehicle and the model that has the economy in the role of facilitating our journeys comprise two cameras filming the same scene. They both depict an entity moving, bringing in questions of speed and ease of motion and success in reaching the destination. In the former, it's the economy cruising or crashing, taking the scenic route or bumbling along. In the latter, the shot tightens and people become the focus of the experience.

By bringing these two models together, progressives can create a comprehensive explanation of the what and the why for our economic framework. Together, they amount to an antidote to the two-model system conservatives have long used to aid their rhetorical cause.

Employing language from both models allows us to begin to undo the deeply damaging ideas explored in the previous chapter: that we are here only to serve the economy and are to remain at its beck and call. This notion of duty, of forsaking all others, even ourselves, to make the economy feel better and get bigger is the conceptual key that's preserved our unsustainable, inequitable, inhumane system.

We must reorient our language and with it our thinking from this way of perceiving and interacting with the world to a much more accurate and just one. Earlier, I depicted this tired old economy as overlord model like this:

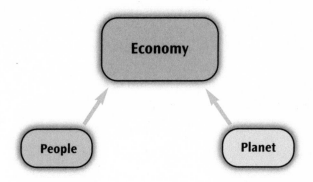

With the help of our new models, we emerge with a new schematic. Here is our relation to the economy when we re-align our perception in accordance with what's true and right in the world.

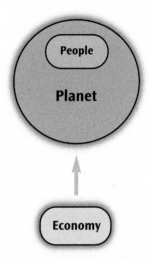

This image depicts the notion that we, in close connection with and reliance upon our natural environment, are what really matters. The economy should be working on our behalf. Judgments about whether a suggested policy is positive or not should be considered in light of how that policy will promote our well-being, not how much it will increase the size of the economy.

Laying the Foundation for Our Case: The Economy as a Constructed Object

Economic messaging relies upon far more than just this handful of models. A topic so complex and colored by political ideology offers a rich range of metaphorical possibilities. There are two other models that emerge frequently enough in common discourse to merit serious attention.

We've already seen that the economy can be readily understood as an object in motion. Here we have a permutation on that theme: the economy as a constructed object. In this model, it's still a thing but a stationary one.

Numerous references appear in economic writing and speech to "building." On the campaign trail in 2007, for example, Obama spoke often of the need to "build the economy from the bottom up" and "rebuild our economy."

Across the ideological divide, Heritage Foundation economic pundit David Mason writes, "Fed Chairman Ben Bernanke suggests that emergency mortgage aid is needed to deal with a situation akin to a fire in the housing markets. Assuming he is correct, is the best time to write a new building code while flames are flaring?"[53]

At the other end, we see frequent references to collapse: "What we're feeling here is the collapse of a house of cards."[54] Similarly, we see references such as "Major institutions have crumbled" and, very commonly, the economy has "caved in."[55]

Language that evokes the economy as a constructed object can't be pinpointed to a specific side of the political spectrum. As we just saw, it's bandied about in left-leaning newspaper editorials and evoked by conservative pundits. We hear on the right that "markets regulated by the rule of law and governed by a freely functioning price system are *post and beam in the architecture* of prosperity."[56] But we also saw Obama using the phrase "new foundation" in his economic discourse so often journalists took to calling it a signature slogan.[57]

When we transfer what we know about built objects onto the far-less-tangible domain of the economy, we get conclusions like the following: economies are created by people; certain components of the economy are fundamental—they serve as a "foundation"; external events, like natural disasters, human error, and bad policymaking, can destroy components of the economy or even the whole thing; and some components or sectors of the economy will last longer than others.

Sounds like a decent framework for laying the conceptual foundation for the economic arguments we'd like to win, doesn't it? On the one hand, it's easy to make the case that we need to let people with experience and expertise manage the economy, just as we wouldn't want to see a high rise go up without the aid of a decent architect and engineers. This certainly holds at the initial stages, when we break ground and build. Also, there's a clear way to argue for government intervention in response to a major calamity; we expect people to step in and fix things when a building is destroyed.

On the other hand, built objects generally don't require daily intervention. This model leaves open to debate which sectors of the economy are well built and can stand alone and which are poorly constructed and deserve renovation or even complete overhaul.

That's the debate we see raging in politics today. All but the most conservative thinkers currently agree that some government action was necessary in 2007 and 2008 given on-the-ground conditions. Opposition to Bush's bank bailout and even Obama's initial stimulus package was far less intense than disapproval for recent budgets, for increasing taxes on the wealthy, and for establishing the Consumer Protection Agency.

People understand the need to tweak the structure, especially after the earthquake and aftershocks we've had; they're far less likely to want to tear things down and start from scratch. Whether or not this model will work for us depends on whether our desired policies are or can be construed as renovations or whether they sound more like demolishing the old and building something new.

Sowing the Seeds for Our Ideas: The Economy as a Crop

Offering up another approach, Robert Reich has painted a picture of the economy as a crop. He has said, for example, "The only resource that's uniquely *rooted* in a national economy is its people."[58] He also tells us, "We're finally *reaping* the whirlwind of widening inequality and ever more concentrated wealth."[59]

Other key progressive organizations, like the labor coalition Rebuild and Renew, use this model in saying that Obama's budget will "sow seeds of a sustainable prosperity" and warn us of the "economic crisis in full bloom."[60] Proponents of so-called green-collar jobs also like to talk about "green shoots" growing from new economic sectors. Ideas of growth, also central to the economy as a body, fit very well in this model.

Note that this language applies to crops specifically, not just to plants in general. We are not describing wildflowers by the side of the road. In other words, there is active human participation in the cultivation and harvest of these fruits.

This metaphor, like all the others, profiles certain facts about the economy. It suggests the economy needs constant, planned, and deliberate tending. It won't yield much left to its own devices. Further, it helps us see that problems in one sector of the economy can spread and contaminate other sectors, just as we know happens in fields.

In addition, this metaphor allows us to speak about the need for experimentation. Many different factors affect the economy; sometimes you need to try different interventions to see what will work. This level of candor would get a politician booed off today's stage. Yet in explaining the reach and design of the New Deal, President Franklin D. Roosevelt declared, "The country needs and, unless I mistake its temper, the country demands bold, persistent experimentation. It is common sense to take a method and try it: If it fails, admit it frankly and try another. But above all, try something."[61]

There's a lot to recommend about this model. It certainly serves the policy objectives of the left more than the right.

Arguing that government has a real and continual role to play—not just as a onetime doctor saving a patient, but as a lifelong steward of our literal daily bread—is facilitated by conceptions of the economy as a kind of crop.

However, it may prove too obscure for practical use. The instances of language suggesting this model are far fewer than the body and object-in-motion models we've already explored. This means that while we can understand references that rely upon thinking of the economy as we would a crop, it's less reliably our automatic tendency to do so. Where we see naturalistic and vehicle models in use to describe everything from hardship to success, individual experiences to national concerns, the same can't be said of the economy as a crop. Instead of having many familiar expressions of this framework already at hand, we'd have to come up with language "rooted" in a crop metaphor for all of the economic issues we seek to discuss.

This brings us to a critical truth about simplifications: we can't invent them from scratch. There are many ways to make sense of a complex abstraction, but there is not an infinite set of readily relied upon options. When deliberately crafting arguments, we must choose, from among those our minds readily grasp, the single metaphor or few models that best highlight what messages we want to foreground.

If I try to talk to you about "the ingredients of a tasty economy," I'd get nothing but blank stares. The notion of likening the economy to food isn't a simplification our brains naturally produce. Attempts to employ this metaphor would simply fall flat. Picking a model from the wide array of those already in use is a required first step in crafting effective messages. Only by doing so can we call up and reinforce the frameworks that advance what we know to be true.

MIXING OUR METAPHORS, MUDDLING OUR MESSAGE

Unlike conservatives, progressives have never been subscribers to one particular model in the communication we create. That would be too easy for us. We seem to be fans of everything under the sun. In fact, swapping one implicit understanding for another in short order is endemic in progressive writing, speech making, and advocacy.

To be fair, this is completely normal. Our brains are wired to grasp multiple models; otherwise many of the things we say to each other wouldn't make sense. But when we are *crafting* communication—not speaking the thoughts as they come into our head—we'd do well to borrow a lesson from conservatives and make our metaphors do the explanatory job that we want.

Just for illustration, I'll continue to pick on EPI: "The upcoming *recovery* package is a critical step in getting the economy *moving again* and *laying the foundation* for future *growth*."[62]

Jumping from body to vehicle to building back to body in one line isn't just bad style; it also risks making it seem we don't know what the economy is—especially when our opponents do a remarkable job of avoiding this kind of talk. In transmitting that there's no consistency or logic to how we make sense of this topic, we undercut our ability to convey our message: that we know this economy thing inside and out and that we can be trusted to handle it.

This tendency toward model switching is all too common. Consider, as another example, this passage from journalist David Leonhardt that goes from body to object in motion: "Ever since Wall Street bankers were called . . . to deal with the *convulsions* in the mortgage market, the economy *has been lurching* from one crisis to the next."[63] Similarly, in the words of his colleague Paul Krugman, "When a stock market bubble and a credit boom *collapsed, bringing down* much of the banking system with them, the Fed *tried to revive the economy* with low interest rates."[64]

It's not hard to see why metaphor mixing is a bad idea. Just as you would run from a doctor who declares a faulty carburetor the cause of your stomach pains, it's hard to credit an "expert" who can't even seem to describe what she's working on. If you don't convey you know what the economy is, how do you expect to convince others that the results of the policies you're arguing for will occur as you claim?

EPI, Leonhardt, and Krugman are in esteemed company here. President Obama, so often touted as a master communicator, frequently veers inexplicably from one explanation of the economy to another. In the earlier years of his term, while drumming up support for the stimulus, among other early policies, he seemed a fan of the building model. Many of his public statements revolved around "pillars of growth" and "sustainable foundations." More recently, however, his speechwriters seem to have lost all track of what they'd have us assume the economy is. Sometimes they'll even have him switch over to reaffirming laissez-faire mythology. Sadly, such statements reinforce the idea that the market will create the most riches, some of which will eventually reach the workers making things go.

At a speech on June 3, 2011, in Toledo, Ohio, celebrating the success of the much-ballyhooed bailout of American automakers, Obama started off well. He offered us glimpses of the vehicle metaphor by saying the economy was on "a bumpy road."[65] Capitalizing on his surroundings, a Chrysler plant, the president added in other choice examples of this understanding to round out his speech, "There are always going to be bumps on the road to recovery. We're going to pass through some rough terrain that even a Wrangler would have a hard time with."[66] This kind of talk helps audiences understand the need for someone to "steer" us toward sustainable prosperity—a valuable idea to establish in explaining just why the government saw fit to spend massively to prop up a sector many conservatives deemed unworthy of a second glance.

But then, in this same speech (and subsequent others), the president abandoned the useful explanation of the economy as a human-made machine only to personify it. Obama explained that economic improvement would require more time by saying, "Just like if you have a bad illness . . . it's going to take a while for you to mend, and that's what's happening to our economy."[67]

But there's no germ or natural disaster behind our recession. What's "happening to our economy" is the result of bad decisions made over time by people and by leaders we elected to know better.

Our economic problem isn't a virus. It results from conscious choices—among them giving money to millionaires who don't need it instead of hiring workers who desperately do. It comes from allowing basic necessities like health care to eat away at earnings instead of putting limits on the profits extracted from illness and injury. And it's refusing to recognize that America is not broke; it's broken—and we'll need to plan and (gasp!) spend money to fix it.

Worse yet, these decisions continue. Leaders from both sides seem intent on inflicting further damage on the economy, which really means on us. Not that we'd ever hear them fess up to this. Still, we're the suckers who can't get out of this thing even as we accelerate toward our own destitution.

Since our economy is not at all like a body, there's no chance it will just magically "mend." And believing it will or telling the public this is so negates the case economists are making for government to stop mass public worker layoffs and cease cuts to basics for the poorest among us.

Recognizing the foolishness of current no-taxing-the-rich, deficit-slashing mania doesn't require advanced training in economics, only a minimum familiarity with basic math. Curbing joblessness by laying people off is like improving gas mileage by puncturing a car's tires.

Granted, Obama and all the others I've chided for falling into bad messaging habits also return time and again to better metaphors. But briefly taking up the vehicle model in the midst of a larger speech isn't enough. Like far too many other Democrats and even self-declared progressives, the comparison of the economy to a body or an aspect of nature has become like a tic that keeps appearing in President Obama's economic discourse.

The ways that left-of-center politicians and advocates shoot themselves in the foot are clear. They employ models that evoke conservative beliefs to make arguments for progressive economic solutions, they switch within an argument or even a single sentence between multiple models, and they imbue the economy with agency and intentionality, obscuring the roles people play and the harms done to them.

All of these commonplace habits reinforce self-defeating notions about the market as an independent entity. This makes it harder to see the truth: the economy is a construction of human choices that requires our oversight and control. We are not here in its service, at its beck and call. It is neither our creator nor our crotchety uncle but rather the means by which we produce and distribute all we need and want in our lives.

Our best hope of evoking the truth is to speak about the economy as an object in motion and, more specifically, as a vehicle. And alongside this, we must convey the message that its purpose is to enable and ease our individual and collective way on the journey of life. Much of the rest, as we'll soon see, is (talking about) history.

CHAPTER 3

Don't Call It a Crisis

Every great mistake has a halfway moment, a split second when it can be recalled and perhaps remedied.
—PEARL S. BUCK, *WHAT AMERICA MEANS TO ME*

Talking about the economy effectively, so that the merits of proven policies like progressive taxation, government investment, and financial regulation become obvious, is no small feat. We've already seen that doing so requires us to clarify our story of what the economy is and how it operates, homing in especially on what we evoke with our metaphors and imply with our too often passive voices. As we explored in the last chapter, we lose the argument before it begins by conveying assumptions at odds with what we emphatically declare. Without staying, so to speak, on metaphor, our arguments about policy particulars prove incoherent.

Memorizing the recommended models is not so hard. It's putting them to work for us that's difficult. And it isn't enough to merely discipline ourselves to consistently use language that calls up one or a few desired underlying models. There are changes to our standard messaging habits required beyond this. If we truly want the public to understand how we got into this mess and approve of our suggestions for extracting ourselves from it, we need to tell a credible, compelling story about how the world does and should work, financially speaking. Stories, as we know from Shakespeare and Hollywood, have heroes and villains, journeys and resolutions, origins and ends. We've generally missed narrating some or all of these elements in our economic policy arguments.

In this chapter, I'll examine how we've been telling the story about the years leading up to and following 2008—the critical moment when our current economic predicament came lumbering into plain and undeniable view. Embedded in most Americans' memories of this sad tale are core assumptions about what makes our economy work well and what causes serious damage.

Shifting the storyline about the origin of our most recent problems is required to change our fundamental assumptions about markets, profit, banking, ownership, and debt. As we will explore, one common strategy for doing this is to engage in comparison to other nations. After examining why this hasn't proven an effective approach, we will then dissect more closely how the explanation of what caused our recession is deeply politicized—a choose your own adventure based on ideology, not facts. Looking more closely at the progressive version of events, otherwise known as reality, we'll examine the most common expressions related to our current hard times, exposing the underlying issues with a whole set of phrases, such as "economic crisis," "financial reform," and "financial sector." By this chapter's end, we will also learn how to walk the tricky line between blaming government for its role in abetting the financial meltdown and touting government as the solution to it at the same time.

THE GRASS IS GREENER, AND THE WORKDAYS ARE SHORTER

One way we can try to tell the tale of what went wrong here and what ought to be is by comparing the way things (don't) work in the United States to life economic in other places. Unfortunately, it's a method that's never proven very effective. Despite this, our attraction to invoking international comparisons and the source of its limitations bear unpacking, as this will inform how we craft a storyline that actually makes sense and persuades.

The impetus behind this approach is a sound one. In theory, if people see that there's one way of organizing economic activity that works for many of the world's people—rules governing how products get made and workers are treated, conditions placed on pollutants produced and who pays to clean them up, mechanisms to guard against extreme poverty—the public will then be more inclined to support restructuring our economy along these same lines.

This line of persuasion would have Americans see that the grass (in many patches) is indeed greener. Believe it or not, there are places where people don't work tirelessly their whole lives only to find themselves one ailment or layoff away from cardboard-box living. Various European countries make great object lessons in what's wrong with America. France spends less on health care with better overall outcomes. Germany takes regulating carbon emission more seriously and reaps the benefit of cleaner air in most of the country. And everywhere else in the world with paved roads and flush toilets, residents work fewer hours than we do.

This sales pitch seems like it should work. Embracing the Yankee can-do spirit, Americans would look around at the world's best practices, appropriate what works, paint it red, white, and blue, and call it our great idea in the first place.

However in practice, this has proven about as effective as a kid cajoling his parents to do something by arguing, "But Madison's parents let her do it!" We haven't gotten very far by insisting, "But France lets its workers have paid sick days!"

Obviously, the current Greek debt debacle and corollary crisis make Europe seem a somewhat less compelling success story. Indicators of health and well-being are still better across the Atlantic, but it's a little hard to point to Europe today as an example for how to structure economic activity. Scandinavia, aka Northern, or non-EU, Europe, can still credibly claim to get this economy management thing right—well, at least, more right than we do. But since many Americans can't even find Alaska on a map, Greece might just as well be a province of Norway.

But even without more recent European economic troubles, allegiance to American exceptionalism runs strong. This comparison-to-others approach to advocacy for economic policymaking simply isn't very effective. Savvier audiences deny any comparison is viable. Some will always claim that what's good for the European is irrelevant for the American. Michael

Moore's documentary *Sicko*, for example, attempted to redeem the much-reviled "socialized medicine" by showing us the inner workings of medical care in France. The result? Virtually nothing but more restaurants changing their menus to say that they served "freedom fries."

To most Americans, this country is simply different from every other place on earth. For many of our people, no foreign nation could ever hold a candle to the homeland. Whatever is happening abroad *obviously* must entail some suppression of freedom or curtailing of growth. How else does anyone explain why other systems didn't give rise to the most prosperous nation not just today but in all of history? Comparisons to other countries, even while they could boast the best of times, have never been particularly moving to us.

We'd need a lengthy digression into our collective psychology to explore the reasons behind our American-itis. Here's one quick fact to clue us in: credible estimates indicate no more than about 35 percent of U.S. citizens currently hold a valid passport, and this figure is reportedly at a record high.[1] Even if we grant the legitimate financial constraints behind this statistic, a significant number of Americans who could afford it prefer never to venture outside of our borders.

This extends, not incidentally, to members of Congress; at last credible count 30 percent of them can't travel past Tijuana or Toronto.[2] Lots of these folks have the money to fly first class, but when it comes to leaving America, they're simply not interested. (Keep in mind, unless you like sleeping well, that 100 percent of these same members get to vote on our foreign policy.)

The story of how the economy operates is one of the few things we've never been keen to import from abroad. Nor has credible proof from other nations convinced us that we could and should structure our economy differently. Fond as we are of the stuff made outside our borders, we're not eager to import the rules and incentives that govern how that stuff gets made.

If we're to change the way Americans think about our economy, we need a homemade explanation for how it came to be structured, its purpose and current operation, where the roads diverged in the wood, and how to get back and take the path to shared prosperity.

THE ORIGIN STORY AND THE FALL

Like any decent explanation, a fully convincing and energizing narrative of what our economy is and how it works must begin with an origin story. But even covering *where do economies come from*—and we haven't—would take us only so far. We not only need to convey the fundamentals, but we also must articulate the recent fall from grace because it was this descent, as we saw earlier, that actually made people wake up and want answers about how the economy functions. This, despite the passage of time and anemic recovery, is still an entry point to a credible argument that something very big is wrong with business as usual.

An accurate description of how we recently got to the brink brings with it an implicit critique of how the system ought to be structured. It also offers a palpable illustration of all that's at stake when we fail at this critical endeavor. And as we saw in the last chapter, what is implied instead of directly asserted can be incredibly powerful.

If we convey, for example, the whole "crisis" was a fluke or an unavoidable cyclical blip, this suggests one set of recommended government actions. Shortly speaking, it implies the best course is no action at all.

Alternatively, we could portray our economic problems as a series of stupid and even nefarious errors—bad decisions made by people elected to know better on behalf of elites paying them to pretend they don't. The economic crisis as fall from grace story is an essential part of explaining where we went wrong and what to do instead.

Just as the story of the flood in Genesis warns religious people about the dangers of ignoring God's dictates, a proper telling of where things went horribly wrong with the economy sets the foundation for our rendering of how things ought to be. Like any good story, there are multiple ways to tell it; the devil is in the details. As expected, we see wrangling over what this tale should be: the moral of the current versions in popular telling depends on who's narrating. Let's explore, in short form, differing takes on what caused what we've come to call the crisis.

The Fall: A Story Told by Conservative Myth-Makers

What caused the recent downturn, according to conservatives? Government. Did you really need to ask? More specifically, the crisis came from meddling, liberal-minded lawmakers intent on social engineering despite the far superior wishes and wisdom of the market.

In this case the economic sin was the attempt to increase access to homeownership through new requirements that more mortgages financed by government-sponsored enterprises such as Fannie Mae and Freddie Mac go to low- and moderate-income buyers. The more specific culprit generally named? In 1977, Congress passed the Community Reinvestment Act (CRA) to end rampant racial discrimination in lending known commonly as redlining. The CRA required banks insured by the government (basically all of them) to provide credit in all communities, not just pick and finance in the white ones. Horrifying, I know!

Congress then voted to beef up the CRA in the 1990s. And as the story goes, this forced Fannie and Freddie to lower underwriting standards in an attempt to get poor people into homes of their own. In short, government rulemaking created demand for unreliable lending products. Next stop: faith-based mortgages and then defaults of massive proportions. Conservative commentator Rick Santelli even coined a catchy phrase for what he saw as a government-induced loan debacle: "losers' mortgages."[3] That'll teach us to try extending the American Dream to . . . Americans!

Never mind that the bipartisan Financial Crisis Inquiry Commission (FCIC) spent fifteen months investigating the causes of the meltdown and came, quite predictably, to a very different conclusion. Citing actual evidence, for example, although Fannie and Freddie operated in America only, lax lending, overvaluation, and the subsequent housing bubble and breakdown actually happened the world over, FCIC didn't find government the principal culprit. Further, the FCIC determined, although Fannie and Freddie certainly jumped on the crap-mortgage bandwagon, the all-stars on Wall Street were the inventors and drivers of this new train of lending. But as humorist Arnold Glasgow used to say, "The fewer the facts, the stronger the opinions."

Conservatives' blame government/poor Wall Street version of events didn't move many people when it first surfaced. But in response to Occupy Wall Street and as part of the Republican presidential primary, it returned with Freddy Krueger vengeance.

Another sequel we didn't need; this story is baaaack. From diehards like Newt Gingrich to supposed moderates like New York mayor Michael Bloomberg, politicians once again want us to believe that the banking sector was the victim, not the cause, of the crisis. In response to Occupy Wall Street, Bloomberg declared, "It was not the banks that created the mortgage crisis. It was, plain and simple, Congress who forced everyone to go and give mortgages to people who were on the cusp."[4]

The genius (let's give credit where due) of conservatives is in not just trumpeting their version of events. They also embed the key ideas that (1) government activity is the problem and (2) economic fluctuations of this magnitude are normal and expected. In fact, as we've already seen, they root this in the very structure of their sentences. They're the masters of the power of presupposition: implying something is true without needing to assert it overtly.

Consider, for example, American Enterprise Institute's article entitled "Ten Ways to Do Better in the Next Financial Cycle."[5] Without bothering to prove its case, the institute is telling us right in the title to *expect another downturn*. In other (and many more) words, this is just the way things go. In more hyperbolic terms, the complete or partial ruination of our economic system should be taken as a given.

There's another villain in the conservative story. The fallible individual is just as culpable as Fannie and Freddie. People were out of control, spending beyond their means and buying what they shouldn't have. Never mind that folks like George W. Bush sold us on the notion of an "ownership society." He likely first used this phrase in a 2003 speech in Kennesaw, Georgia, to rally support for a tax-cut proposal.[6] Its meaning ultimately extended throughout his two terms to become associated with homeownership, along with the idea that health care, savings, and education were really best left to each individual to manage.

Nevertheless, according to the popular conservative retelling of the crisis tale, it was avarice, not pride, that went before the financial fall. Financial institutions were not only blameless; some even believe they were the ones hurt. Other victims included the *good* people who didn't buy more than they could afford.

This reading of recent history isn't just wonky economic musing—it can determine future policy. Reacting to an Obama plan to reduce the principal owed on certain underwater mortgages, Republican Senator Bob Corker (TN) spelled out his disapproval for certain homeowners. He said, "People who acted responsibly in Tennessee will be paying for the bad behavior of [other] lenders and borrowers."[7]

The moral of Corker's reading of the crisis couldn't be clearer: government should always do less, and the individual is clearly to blame for what befalls her. Welcome back the economy as a moral enforcer.

Our Version of the Tale

So how have we been describing the housing bubble, market collapse, and Great Recession? And what tales do we tell about events that preceded it: most importantly, the Gilded Age to Great Depression to New Deal?

You won't be surprised to hear that we've spilled lots of ink on this topic—offering up detailed examinations of every policy turn, regulation overhaul, and financial sector malfeasance. Take, for example, Nobel Prize winner Joseph Stiglitz's brilliant account, "Anatomy of a Murder: Who Killed the American Economy?"[8] He gives us the whole breakdown; but it takes him twelve pages, and he embeds the idea of the economy as a body in the very title of this complicated rendering. Or consider just some of the excellent volumes our side has produced on this question: *This Time Is Different*, *How Markets Fail*, and *Freefall*.[9] Obviously, conservatives have written whole books on the subject as well. But they can also answer "what caused the crisis" in a word: government. We need to say a whole lot more to any audience—no matter if this causes people to stop listening.

Length is really only one dimension of our problem, a proxy for my contention that we don't have a clear story to tell. For illustration and to be fair, Krugman did offer this one sentence summation in an interview; "Regulation didn't keep up with the system."[10] But, again, what does this tell us about who is the actor and who is acted upon? Moreover, it is once again an implicit critique of government—the very agent Krugman and other progressives are arguing we need to put in charge of righting these wrongs.

On the right, a single-word answer transmits all of this because conservatives have done the requisite background work of vilifying government and letting us know the economy is best left on its own.

We're also intent on using historical comparison when we don't try the international approach described before. If you're on Facebook, you've likely seen one of many graphics demonstrating the extent of inequality today and how it mirrors wealth distribution just before the Great Depression.

These kinds of depictions are startling and compelling to many people. I know because dozens of them have sent them to me. They're meant as a visual story of what caused the recession, offering an explanation far deeper than citing lax lending standards or naming a few bad apples in finance. They show, not just tell, us that there's something fundamentally destabilizing about huge concentrations of wealth—especially, for those who dig a bit deeper, in an economy so dependent upon consumer spending. These kinds of charts generally appear with their siblings and cousins—visuals documenting, for example, what a CEO makes compared to an average worker and diminishing wage gains despite increased productivity.

But all of these graphs, well done and researched as they are, don't work without a foundation of belief behind them. They require us to already get what the economy is. The facts they present —namely, inequality was pronounced before the Great Depression and is again now—don't place the murder weapon in the suspect's possession. Because, again, we haven't even established that human action, not divine will or natural disaster, is at the root of economic outcomes.

Just as we need to define how the economy operates, that it's a thing people made and must control, leaving the origins of the current recession murky is not an option for us. When our side of the story isn't audible, the conservative take on things becomes the default.

Scholar john a. powell[11] articulates the danger of letting conservatives' renderings, especially versions charging ordinary people, stand: "We have focused once again on what was wrong with the blacks and Latino communities and not on what was wrong with the credit system. . . . Our unwillingness to tell a different, more accurate story means that our structures have largely remained unfixed. *We have convicted the wrong person(s) and the real criminal remains at large.*"[12]

Investor and *Washington Post* columnist Barry Reinholz also captures the power of seizing the origin story. He calls recent attempts to rewrite the history of the financial collapse "the Big Lie." After describing multiple contemporary tall tales, he says, "Wall Street has its own version: Its Big Lie is that banks and investment houses are merely victims of the crash. You see the entire boom and bust was caused by misguided government policies. It was not irresponsible lending or derivative or excess leverage or misguided compensation packages, but rather long-standing housing policies that were at fault."[13] In the face of these dangerous alternate tales we can't rely on our visuals to speak for themselves, not when we don't embed them in a relevant story.

The Crisis of Our Critique

Worse yet, we dilute their potential impact with some of the words we most commonly use to describe what went down. "Economic crisis" as a label for what happened crept into policy circles, news media, and popular discourse in late 2008 and stuck stubbornly. Google trends shows that from this time until the summer of 2009 use of this term shot up. Add in the closely related "financial crisis," which ascended even higher but became less popular far more rapidly, and it's worth probing just what we're telling people in calling this thing that happened a crisis.

In other words, what does a crisis, as the term is more commonly used, really mean?

cri·sis

> 1 a : the turning point for better or worse in an acute disease or fever b : a paroxysmal attack of pain, distress, or disordered function c : an emotionally significant event or radical change of status in a person's life <a midlife *crisis*>
>
> 2 : the decisive moment (as in a literary plot)
>
> 3 a : an unstable or crucial time or state of affairs in which a decisive change is impending; *especially* : one with the distinct possibility of a highly undesirable outcome <a financial *crisis*> b : a situation that has reached a critical phase <the environmental *crisis*>[14]

The word *crisis* alone already frames the economic situation. And it captures much of what we need the public to understand. The notion that a "decisive change is impending" calls us to believe we won't tolerate the status quo much longer. Cue the protestors in Madison, Occupy Wall Street, and elsewhere across the country carrying this banner.

However, crisis also brings with it other implications that are potentially problematic. We often think about crises as sudden, unpredictable turns of events. Think of the common usages of this concept, like *midlife crisis* and *identity crisis*. These are generally unanticipated alterations of behavior. Uncle Louie quit his lifelong job at the laboratory; Mom bought a totally impractical car. We never saw that coming. Not at all the way we'd expect that person—or in the case of the economy, thing—to behave.

Furthermore, with midlife and identity crises, we don't necessarily look for a solution to emerge from a studied course of intervention, nor are we out looking for someone to blame for what happened. In fact, we might be tempted to believe the situation will right itself. Eventually, the unexpected alteration will become a distant, if still painful, memory.

This is, of course, very far from an accurate portrait of what happened. By extension, it muddies what we need people to understand about the economy more broadly. What those of us who favor things like the financial transaction tax and regulation are trying to make clear is that a long series of pathetically conscious decisions and, to be fair, some unintended mistakes preceded the shit hitting the fan. The economy did not up and decide to dye its hair pink after sporting a lifelong, respectable, chestnut-hued bob.

Similarly, since our economic problems won't just sort themselves out, implying this is the case, as *crisis* likely does, undermines our cause. It becomes very difficult to argue for careful scrutiny and improved future policymaking if such events just happen from time to time, regardless of our behavior.

To be sure, there is another understanding of crisis as something that builds over time, reaches a critical point, and requires skilled attention. This, as in the third definition above, is most noticeable in the usage *environmental crisis*. While this could refer to an oil spill, it more commonly means steady deterioration over a long period. It implies a requirement for deliberate remedy.

Consider, for illustration, the following other nouns that I'd prefer to see used with "economic":

1. damage
2. delusion
3. blunder

Sound awkward? They should. These phrases aren't the way we're used to hearing people describe the events of 2007–2008. But recall it or not, there was likely a time when "war on terror" sounded as foreign as "war on anger" does now. Through repetition, however, we come to accept even the idea that you can send in an army to fight a feeling.

It's difficult to say, short of conducting a sociolinguistic experiment, which meaning of crisis (sudden, unanticipated, self-correcting event versus gradual, deliberate process needing intervention) is more closely attached to economic crisis. Examining popular usage of the word, however, suggests we most often use it to convey the earlier version. Thus, our frequent reliance on the phrase "economic crisis" most likely does not establish the necessary idea that this was a long time coming, people in power made it happen, and we need to act deliberately to change course.

If we assume, as I'm suggesting we should, that calling current events in our economy a crisis means we're conveying notions of suddenness and self-correction, then we should try some of the less familiar phrases above instead. But, of course, no two-word descriptor, no matter how catchy, will do all of our explanation for us. Any phrase we come up with works only when it fits into, calls up, and unconsciously reinforces the broader explanation we have already offered.

Wall Street as Naughty Schoolboy

Crisis is far from the only word we need to think harder about before using so liberally. Our cries for change post-2008 are generally framed under the broad heading "financial reform." It's worth interrogating what this construction implicitly tells audiences.

In English, we reform naughty schoolboys by sending them to special schools. In doing so, we mean to convey that they've established a pattern of behaving very badly. Numerous, less extreme options like losing recess and suspension have failed to yield the desired change in behavior—so harsher punishment is the only remaining solution.

A word like "reform" implies the entity subject to this process is something intractable. Consider a notion that loomed large in the 1990s: "welfare reform." This was the brainchild of the Clinton administration that even staunch conservatives grudgingly admit to loving. By describing welfare as something needing reform, leaders implied it was inherently problematic. Contrast this frame, for the sake of illustration, with "welfare improvement" or the neutral options of "welfare alteration" and "welfare change." Each phrase tells us powerfully different tales about what welfare is and what ought to be done to it. Sadly, every time those of us opposing gutting vital services for needy families repeated the phrase "welfare reform," we actually reaffirmed that the program was a problem, even as we fought vigorously for its preservation.

In one sense, then, "financial (sector) reform" is the perfect phrase. Unlike welfare, finance is something that's proven itself incredibly naughty. But the term may not go far enough to convey what's at stake and the full scale of dysfunction we're asking to have corrected.

Reform technically means to reshape or refashion from existing materials. It suggests less a complete overhaul than a tinkering at the edges of something not right.

As such it's a completely accurate description of the aims behind what we've accomplished to date. For example, the Dodd-Frank bill brought some measure of regulation to financial firms and created the Consumer Protection Agency. Arguably, even measures not yet enacted like the financial transaction tax and reinstatement of Glass-Steagall would fit comfortably under the banner of reform. None of these are intended to alter the basic business of Wall Street. Instead, they are designed to reassert some control over the rampant speculation, double-dealing, and profit-seeking that helped bankers extract money for wrecking our economy. So reform is a fair label for them.

The question progressives must ask themselves is this: Do we want government to have increased powers to regulate what happens on Wall Street, or do we want to seriously reconsider the purpose and operations of our financial systems? Put another way, do we seek to just bring banking to heel, or do we intend to fundamentally reconsider what it is and how it operates?

These are two very different missions. Enacting, or more accurately restoring, additional government oversight to financial transactions would still keep financial firms operating largely as usual. Demanding, instead, that corporations not be considered people, curtailing possible campaign contributions, eliminating exotic financial products, and instituting other such policies would radically alter the purpose and operation of banking.

Cries for reform seem adequate to describing the first task. However, they're not up to the job of the second. Notice, for example, that Occupy Wall Street and its spin-offs rarely (if ever) champion the need for financial reform. Theirs is a much more ambitious agenda.

Some chalk this up to the purported and much criticized lack of any clear demands whatsoever. But this notwithstanding, these protestors clearly aren't crying out for some alterations at the edges. In awakening the world to our vast and egregious inequalities and demanding we get money out of politics, they're seeking far more than some shifting at the margins.

In contrast, with "financial reform" as our goal statement, we confine ourselves entirely to the inner workings of banking and related activities. We aren't, as the Occupy movement would have us, critiquing the tight connection between Wall Street and Washington, K Street, and Congress. Our statement remains silent and therefore arguably approving of the inexcusable purchase of policy via campaign contributions. Overturning *Citizens United*, for example, doesn't quite fit under the banner of financial reform. But it's a clear part of a set of objectives framed more broadly as reshaping this portion of our economy and how it influences rulemaking.

Again, purely to highlight the contrast, here are some other pithy names I'd prefer for what we seek—some of which are already in common usage:

1. Financial overhaul
2. Consumer protection[15]
3. Make banking boring[16]

It's worth sidetracking to note that the word *occupy* itself offers us two potential meanings. The more obvious one is to inhabit or take up residency. This is what we think of when we see the camping supplies in Oakland, Los Angeles, Portland, and elsewhere. Additionally, *occupy* means to be kept busy—as in "That boy needs to be occupied; he's hyperactive." I'd argue that those tent-dwelling protestors at Zuccotti Park were among the very few folks "occupied" in anything productive within the vicinity of Wall Street.

This theme deserves much wider articulation. It's closely related to Paul Krugman's idea of making banking boring. In other words, our financial elite have stopped contributing meaningfully to the economy. Instead of adding in value, the way providing capital for new investments does, it has turned to profiting off dismantling what's come to be called the "real economy."

Because of my work examining how people make sense of the economy, I was asked to be involved in creating a presentation for a teach-in on November 9, 2011, on what caused our recession and what needs to be done. Organized by the grassroots coalition Rebuild the Dream in partnership with pioneer online campaigner MoveOn, the slide show presentation went out to thousands of people through house parties and described a series of stark differences between the world as the 1% engineers it and the world as it ought to be.

These differences make up the truths that we need to internalize before we can enunciate a coherent vision and call to economic action. Teach-in presentation creator, Ryan Senser, and I labeled one of these creating an economy based on *making things versus making things up*. This contrast reaches straight to the heart of what's wrong with finance as it currently stands.

Many economists have written of more dangers to come stemming from the decline of American manufacturing and the growth of finance as an increasingly large percentage of our economy. The danger is that the latter quite literally doesn't make anything. At least not things we can eat, heat homes with, or use to survive. At some point, generating concentrated wealth by syphoning it from the productive economy won't be an option. Once the parasite sucks all the blood from its host, there's nothing left for it to live on.

Yet despite some incredible new ideas and solutions economists have crafted for retooling our economy, Americans have not really examined one of the huge questions of our day. Namely, how a functional, nonpolluting, non-resource-extracting, somewhat equitable U.S. economy ought to be structured. Foremost here is the issue of how we reorient away from our precarious reliance on consumer spending. Of equal importance is a question not even contemplated: What is the functional, productive use of storing and moving money? This is what I'd begin to call a desirable role for the big bad high priests of Wall Street.

We'll turn to this issue in depth in the concluding chapter, examining the big new economic ideas and asking the questions we need answered to truly create an economic system that works worldwide for all people. In the meantime, let's get back to the issue of language. How do we set up receptivity for this much larger and long overdue conversation about how the economy ought to be? We must first take care to accurately convey what finance is in the present.

Give Less Credit to Wall Street

When we consider how little Wall Street produces, it seems far too kind to keep referring to it as a part of something called the financial sector. Former Goldman Sachs midlevel executive Greg Smith may have caused quite a stir in revealing in a *New York Times* op-ed the complete absence of ethics at his firm, but insiders' responses show that the surprise wasn't the goings-on but the fact that anyone would dare to talk about them publicly. The surprise wasn't *what* he told but *that* he told.

By calling the surreal world of finance a "sector," we inadvertently put it on equal footing with real components of our economy—say, for example, the manufacturing sector or the service sector. This label suggests there's some real, tangible work happening of a relevant purpose. Why? Because a sector is a designation for groups of jobs that keep their workers, well, occupied. It's easy and obvious to name a kind of activity in these other economic categories: hair cutting, car building, teeth cleaning, and on and on. Similarly, it's little trouble to describe the outputs and useful contributions of each effort.

The useful role of finance is to act as a middleman. Its job is to transfer capital from folks who want to save it to those who want to put it to more immediate productive uses. This plus convenience—I, for one, don't want to carry around wads of easily lost, easily stolen cash—is what banking is good for. And while this still isn't as tangible as making a table or teaching geometry, it's not grounds to send anyone to white-collar prison. In fact, it's actually helpful for the economy overall and the individuals in it.

But this useful stuff forms a smaller and smaller portion of what the banksters "employed" in finance spend their time doing. Bundling together what's worthless and declaring it valuable and betting against their own investments—such actions done in other contexts could be called racketeering. Just stick well-tailored suits on the players, and we call it banking.

As a name, *finance* is fine—without the sector. *Money management* might be a bit better—it gives bankers something to try to actually accomplish. *Moneylending* is another choice—it's the one I think Jesus would have liked, right before he advised us to kick them out of the temple of national influence on decisionmaking and governance. But *financial sector* lends legitimacy where none is due. Given finance's current reluctance to provide loans to us, the last thing we need to do is dole credit the banks' way.

GOVERNMENT AS HERO AND VILLAIN

Sorting through the most effective ways to convey our assumptions about the causes of the recession overall and the specifics of what finance did and should be doing is tricky enough. On top of this, we have the added challenge of presenting an effective message about the role of government.

Don't get me wrong; there's much blame to heap on government for our current situation. We've seen conservatives argue that it did too much, while progressives try to make the case that it did too little. Either way, the arguments boil down to condemnation of government's efficacy.

Add to this the massive issues of close connections between regulators and the industries they purport to watch over and the campaign contributions that help sway lawmakers toward corporate interests, and you've got a big pile of sins to lay at government's door.

Yet many of the arguments progressives seek to make rest upon having government do more. This is a hard sell in the best of circumstances. We make it basically impossible to believe if in setting the stage for this claim, we first convince our audiences that government can't do anything right.

Thus in detailing where government has failed, we must simultaneously *insist government has an essential role*. This requires we thread a very fine but essential needle for stitching a logical, complete argument.

In the language of the vehicle metaphor we saw earlier, this could be phrased as follows: "Government took its hands off the wheel and our economy crashed, hard." This assumes, without brooking argument, in the future there still has to be a driver. No one hearing of a car crash due to poor driving would then assume we should have cars operate autonomously.

In our narrative of the recent crisis, we must maintain a balance between describing what happened accurately and avoiding vilifying government. Especially to the degree we then can't redeem it. Here are some strategies for doing so without undercutting the progressive message:

1. Describe as the problem past administrations/leaders, not government overall.

2. Admit government didn't do the best job recently but has in the more distant past and will in the future because of lessons learned.

3. Attribute recent government failing to structural issues (e.g., securities became so complex that regulators charged with oversight couldn't understand, let alone police, them). Thus, highlight the need for transparency and simplification in financial instruments so that government can successfully carry out the job it's charged with completing.

None of these are particularly straightforward, complete, or satisfying. They all leave questions about how exactly we remain so sure government is the solution when it was un-questionably part of creating the problem.

A fourth admittedly difficult but intriguing approach would be to argue not about old government that screwed up versus new government that will clean up but about the dangers of *concentration of power whether in government or outside of it.* This, essentially, is the argument behind the 99% movement.

When too few people have access to power, and worse yet when those few are all old cronies, our political and economic systems become profoundly undemocratic. This makes it hard, if not impossible, for government to act as a check on the market.

But highlighting this fact doesn't lend itself to a neat or feasible conclusion. It is still hard to argue that government should play a continual supervisory role because implicit in this critique is the admission that government today isn't up to that task. It suggests that what's needed is a profound shake-up not just of our economic system but also of our entire notion of participatory democracy.

The question of how to talk about what government is and what role it's to play has no easy answer. As we wrestle with it, we must keep in mind that how we portray government on the cause side will directly influence what we can argue about its role in formulating and enforcing solutions. Meanwhile, as we will explore in the next chapter, progressives face an even more crucial task—articulating the economic problem of our time, which also happens to be a documented source of our economic crisis: our vast and growing inequality of wealth and income.

CHAPTER 4

Do You Think the Poor Are Lazy?

*We can either have democracy in this country or we can
have great wealth concentrated in the hands of a few,
but we can't have both.*

—LOUIS BRANDEIS, QUOTED IN
MR. JUSTICE BRANDEIS: GREAT AMERICAN

We've seen how our imprecision about the nature of the
economy combined with our lack of a clear origin story for
the recession spells communication disaster. But there's one
other big element to our messaging muddle: conveying the
what and the why of income and wealth inequality. As we'll
see in this chapter, our mixed and inaccurate messages about
what inequality is and where it comes from make it hard for
listeners to believe this is a problem of our deliberate creation. This, in turn, inhibits any case that since certain people
made this mess, these guilty parties should get on their hands
and knees and clean it up.

Income and wealth inequality isn't *an* economic problem.
It's *the* economic problem of our time. A diverse array of folks,

including Robert Reich, President Obama, and Harvard Business School professor David Moss, have all made precisely this claim.

Any economy, especially one as much fueled by consumption as ours is today, depends upon having consumers. A vast swath of people buying things in order to employ other people to make those things, as well as to provide services. To buy things and services, these folks need cash. Any policy that funnels money away from poor and middle-class people contributes to the dismantling of the entire economy. Though the well off may be getting more in the process, as my mother likes to say, no matter how rich you are, you still only eat one dinner. We're going to see even more empty restaurants and out of work waiters if fewer of us can pay for our meals.

And the end of Taco Tuesdays is only the beginning. When Harvard economist David Moss overlaid a graph plotting financial deregulation and bank failures against another tracing inequality, he found a stunning near-perfect overlap. While any social scientist worth her tenure wouldn't confuse correlation with causation, we see time and again that letting Wall Street become a dollar-sucking machine makes two giant messes: financial instability and extreme inequality.

Even conservatives grudgingly admit inequality not only exists but also poses a legitimate problem. Neocon icon and *Weekly Standard* author Mathew Continetti wrote, "When Paul Krugman writes that 'extreme concentration of income is incompatible with real democracy,' he has a point. . . . The Founders of this nation also understood the problematic relation between democracy and inequality."[1] House Budget chairman Paul Ryan managed to affirm publicly that responsibility for footing the tax bill had shifted from the wealthiest quintile to the suckers outside of it.[2] When we consider the core ideology of these sources, these otherwise pathetic admissions of reality are on par with the pope becoming a spokesman for Trojans®.

Clearly, inequality has become part of the national conversation. And since progressives know inequality is our leading economic problem, it's critical to ask, what do Americans generally believe about it?

IN 2005, PSYCHOLOGISTS Michael Norton and Dan Ariely went digging into how Americans think about inequality. They asked a nationally representative sample of 5,522 folks to select their ideal from three possible scenarios of wealth distribution: full equality, actual figures in the United States, and current levels in Sweden. Only 10 percent of people preferred to live in an off-kilter society like our own. In contrast, 43 percent selected full equality as their preferred scenario, with 47 percent picking slight inequality like Sweden's.[3]

The researchers then asked everyone to guess at the actual distribution of wealth in our nation. Participants believed that the richest quintile owned 50 percent of the nation's wealth. In reality, at the time of the experiment, that wealthiest fifth clung tightly to no less than 84 percent of our money. And where participants favored a distribution that would make us Nordic, according to the CIA World Fact Book, we *actually* sit squarely between such leading lights as Bulgaria and Cameroon when it comes to how concentrated income is in just a few hands.

To say we're in deep denial about the extent and harms of inequality is to say the polar ice caps are getting a bit moist. It's a false and foolish understatement. While Occupy Wall Street has done much to bring the issue out of the shadows and into the headlines, we remain a long way from grasping the magnitude of the problem. And even if we did, it would amount to only the smallest of steps forward.

If we truly wanted to wrestle with our cruel and destabilizing inequality, we'd have to confront its sources. But our blindness to the amount of inequality and its effects on our society isn't a matter of ignorance or apathy. It's at least partly a function of how we talk about the issue.

As I'll illustrate, because of deeply embedded conceptual preferences reinforced by our most commonly used metaphors, it's challenging for people to grasp, let alone focus sustained attention on, the problem of economic inequality. And as should by now be a familiar refrain, elements of this conceptual muddle are actually of our own making. The most routine ways we have of describing the issue make it hard for us to motivate adequate concern and effective action. Fortunately, there are two promising ways to describe inequality—to convey both the problems it causes for the entire economy and the harms it creates for the individuals and groups bearing the brunt of it.

LOSING THE BLAME GAME

Right now, it's all too easy to tell a story about wealth and poverty that pins blame for failure on the individual. Conservatives are reliably transparent on this. Take, for instance, onetime presidential hopeful Herman Cain, who declared, "Don't blame Wall Street, don't blame the big banks, if you don't have a job and you're not rich, *blame yourself*. It is not someone's fault if they succeeded, *it is someone's fault if they failed*."[4]

Newt Gingrich elaborated on his idea to suspend child labor restrictions and have students take a paid turn as school janitors by saying that poor kids have "no habits of working and nobody around them who works."[5] (There's a bonus to this brilliance. By firing the adults currently in these jobs, we could pay their offspring even less to do them!) Speaking on the *Today* show, Mitt Romney dismissed concerns of inequality as an issue of "envy."[6] It's striking that this, of all subjects, is what these bitter rivals agree on.

Forbes contributor Gene Marks caused a stir by proffering a slew of unsolicited advice for poor black kids. In fact, he's produced an article just for them entitled "If I Was a Poor Black Kid." Perhaps first on his list should be to learn how properly to use the subjunctive in English. Nevertheless, he's clearly a great resource as a white guy raised middle class. Among his pearls of wisdom are these: work hard, get good grades, and learn about computers.[7] In short when you fail, it's not us—it's you.

From his perch at the libertarian Cato Institute, P. J. O'Rourke wrote, "If you want a donkey, if you want a meal, if you want an employee, don't complain about what other people have, go get your own. The tenth commandment sends a message to collectivists, to people who believe wealth is best obtained by redistribution. And the message is clear and concise: Go to hell."[8]

Inequality, to hear many folks tell it, is not just a natural side effect of a capitalist economy—it's a desirable benefit. Conservatives have managed to paint inequality as an asset, a helpful aid in improving the economy overall. It's not just wealth that's good, but actual inequality. Here's an example of this logic:

> Bigness in business does not impair, but *improves the conditions of the rest of the people*. The millionaires are acquiring their fortunes in supplying the many with articles that were previously beyond their reach. If laws had prevented them from getting rich, the average American household would have to forego many of the gadgets and facilities that are today its normal equipment. This country enjoys the highest standard of living ever known in history because for several generations no attempts were made toward "equalization" and "redistribution." *Inequality of wealth and incomes is the cause of the masses' well-being*, not the cause of anybody's distress. Where there is a "lower degree of inequality," there is necessarily a lower standard of living of the masses.[9]

Recently, we've heard such notable leaders as Paul Ryan (R-WI), Jon Kyl (R-AZ), and John Boehner (R-OH) assure us that the poverty, foreclosure, and related travails their policies inflict upon families are actually those families' own damn fault. Paul Ryan championed his proposed budget cuts as the way "to ensure that America's safety net does not become a hammock that lulls able-bodied citizens into lives of complacency and dependency."[10]

This ethos doesn't just come from on high. In response to Occupy Wall Street's meme about the 99%, rank-and-file conservatives attempted to fight back by creating a website called "We are the 53%."[11] This reference to the supposed proportion of Americans who pay income taxes features angry individuals narrating their own story of doing it all by themselves. Their message to those who see structural causes behind wealth and income disparity is clear: quit your bitching.

Those of us not in the conservative camp generally offer only slightly better consolation. Where conservatives see personal fault, most others are quick to name misfortune. Poverty is an accident of birth, a twist of fate, a string of bad hands played out over a lifetime.

For example, Whitney Tilson, a director at Democrats for Education Reform, states, "Poor children can accomplish great things in spite of *the cards they have been dealt*."[12] This sentiment is widespread. Nobel laureate in economics James Heckman argues, "The *accident of birth* is the greatest source of inequality."[13] In fact, we commonly call the poor the "less fortunate."

The pesky facts tell a very different story. The poor are neither unmotivated nor unlucky. To put it plainly: they're being screwed. Or, in much more elegant terms, as legal scholar Michelle Alexander names it, the poor, especially people of color, exist in a "closed circuit of perpetual marginality."[14]

Our manufactured inequality problems go far beyond class. As Alexander has ably proven, there's a huge, growing, and generally overlooked racial component. Just do a quick scan of haves and have-nots; it doesn't take long to notice darker skin tones among the latter.

According to the Economic Policy Institute, roughly 25 percent of all U.S. households had no or *negative* net worth in 2009, an unpardonable increase from 18.6 percent in the halcyon days of 2007. But for African Americans, the perilous standing of absolutely no assets or debts that outnumber them rose to nearly 40 percent in 2009. Median net worth for an African American family in that year, $2,200, was the lowest in recorded history. The median white household came in at $97,900—or forty-four times as much.[15]

If so inclined, you can twist this story to fault the individual. (This will be easier if you listen to conservative talk radio.) But when you see numbers not about how things end up but rather about the causes of those outcomes, it becomes harder to maintain these delusions.

Here are some illustrations:

1. Schools with 50 percent or more minority students experience twice the teacher turnover rate as schools with lower minority populations.[16]

2. Lack of sure access to food is more than twice as likely for children of color than for their white peers.[17]

3. Black children are 350 times and Latino children 280 times more likely to live in poverty as white children are.[18]

4. In nineteen states, African Americans are more than twice as likely as whites to live in neighborhoods where air pollution seems to pose the greatest health danger.[19]

If statistics aren't enough to tell this story—and as I keep harping, they're not—let's try common logic: if hard work truly paid off, sweatshop laborers and slaves would be the world's richest people.

Shut out from the opportunities and experiences that make freedom and security possible, the vast majority of people are not suffering from lack of luck or ambition. They are at the receiving end of deliberate malfeasance. Our nation is engaged in a long-running crime: aggravated impoverishment. The victims are clustered in a very specific portion of our population, most notably communities of color.

Yet the prevailing myth of mobility for all persists largely unquestioned. Norton and Ariely's results are but one illustration. Pew Research also reports, "An overwhelming percentage of Americans believe that people who are poor do not succeed because of their own shortcomings[;] only 19% emphasized the roll of discrimination or other structural and economic forces that go beyond the control of any one individual."[20]

Sadly, as the chart on page 112 demonstrates, belief becomes the basis for policy. Plotting the perception of people around the world who believe that luck determines income against social spending as a proportion of GDP, the United States falls near the bottom on both counts. The residents of other countries, Belgium, Sweden, and Denmark, for instance, are far more likely to attribute making a fortune to the whims of good fortune—and they spend to support the less fortunate accordingly. When you assume being rich has to do with external factors, not inherent superiority, it's logical that the converse also makes sense to you. Poverty is attributable to

Belief That Luck Determines Income

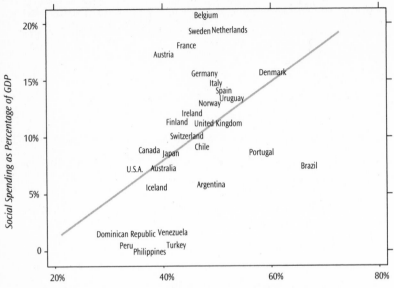

Percentage Who Believe that Luck Determines Income

Source: Alesina, Angeletos, Glaser, and Sacerdote (2003)[21]

conditions, not individual failings. Holding this notion, you're then more likely to approve of and even desire assistance for people born or dropped unceremoniously into hard times.

Ironically, most of the countries that boast this more realistic view of why people end up wealthy actually have a higher degree of mobility. Credible international comparisons demonstrate that in a contest to be crowned land of dreams come true, we're not even runner-up. According to a study from the Organization for Economic Cooperation and Development, the United States sits behind such "anticapitalist" centers as Denmark, Norway, Canada, Sweden, and France in terms of how much a person's eventual net worth is a direct result of where her parents started out.

Why then do Americans remain so intent on believing, despite all available evidence, that this is still the land of opportunity? Why is it so hard for us to grasp that inequality exists, how bad it is right now, and what its origins are? In fact, given the inexcusable outcomes for people of color from colonial times until today, how could any of us have ever believed there was a time when anyone could make it in America by pulling hard enough on his bootstraps?

The Definition Problem

Why is it so hard to "get" inequality? To start, there's difficulty saying what inequality *is*. How much difference and in what areas deserve the label "inequality" make the definitions of this term almost as numerous as the people who seek to define it.

In my conversations with leading progressive economic thinkers, descriptions of inequality began to sound like that obscenity canard "I know it when I see it." Responses ranged from the tautological "the state of not being equal" to the benign "inequality is just differences, and there are ways of measuring differences across populations."

This leaves an opening for a pet conservative take on this issue: there's no inequality problem; the poor are not poor. Just ask Heritage Foundation's Robert Rector, who says, "Most of America's 'poor' live in material conditions that would be judged as comfortable or well-off just a few generations ago."[22] *The Economist*, a widely respected magazine, gets in on this action in an editorial by stating, "The everyday experience of consumption among the less fortunate has become in many ways more like that of their wealthy compatriots."[23]

Libertarians also claim that being rich and being poor are more similar these days. Cato Institute's Will Wilkinson explains why it's actually the rich who are getting a bad deal: "Wealthier Americans . . . [spend] a much larger portion [of their budgets] on services provided by local labor such as home cleaning, lawn care, psychotherapy, and yoga classes. Because the prices of such services are relatively unaffected by the rise of competitive global markets, these landmark developments [i.e., consumer goods are cheaper now] in recent economic history have done less to improve the bang of a wealthy person's buck."[24] There's even a pet name for this development: "democratization of luxury."[25]

Notwithstanding this bizarre vision of poor people watching sitcoms on a flat screen while across town bankers and CEOs struggle to pay for their live-in chefs, effects of inequality are clearly visible to most people. It is the *causes* of inequality that remain very much up for debate. A debate that dictates the viability of solutions each side puts forth, up to and including do nothing at all.

The Abstraction Problem

Faced with differences in the wealth of one group relative to another, we seek explanations. The human brain is wired to latch onto the tangible and shy away from the abstract. Where it's hard to see, feel, hear, and thus have a visceral reaction to concepts such as inequality, lived experience is immediate and well known.

Sadly, the simplest and most concrete explanation is that one group "deserves" riches, while the other doesn't. All of us have the experience of working hard and of slacking off; those of us in positions of privilege have been spared repeated discrimination. And none of our brains can grasp "systemic patterns of unequal treatment." They have no shape or weight.

Despite popular idiom, an apt descriptor of our cognitive system boils down to *I'll see it when I believe it*. We are innate pattern recognizers and want what we believe to hold firm over time. We cannot *see*, largely because we unconsciously elect to ignore, things that do not accord with our preexisting beliefs. Thus, for those who assume differential outcomes are the result of unequal effort or ability, seeing an African American elected president is proof that effort always yields rewards. In other words, racism has gone the way of stonewashed jeans in America.

This poses an immense challenge for discussing inequality. At the outset, inequality is about population-level differences, not individual ones. Further, progressives are arguing it's about differences attributable to systemic flaws, not individual ones.

Conservative opposition to addressing inequality rests on assertions about individuals. Luckily for conservatives, this is where our brains naturally want to go. This makes it easy for them to oversimplify the causes of inequality: "There are two main reasons that American children are poor: their parents don't work much, and fathers are absent from the home."[26] Likewise, they can vividly express their disdain for our concern over inequality: "Individuals who worry overmuch about inequality can succumb to life-distorting envy and resentment."[27]

And they can enunciate a simple critique of just about any solution to inequality that emerges: such policies destroy the incentives that make individuals productive. With the cognitive advantage firmly on their side, it's no wonder conservatives' self-made man story refuses to go out of fashion.

The Acknowledgment Problem

It's news to no one that Americans are scared for our future. Fewer and fewer of us believe things will be better for our children, more distrust government, and practically nobody has faith the economy will ever be as it was.

As public institutions like universities and libraries are allowed (or encouraged) to decay, individuals not only feel the need to fend for themselves; in many cases there are no other options. If you can't stomach your local public school, no wonder you loathe the taxes that fund it. You won't use it for your kids' education, and now you need more money for private school tuition.

This, of course, is a self-fulfilling cycle. As more people leave public systems, these systems further degrade, driving more people to want out. It requires a leap of faith to believe all will work better if you and your loved ones come back into the collective. This requires all the other families on the block to think this way as well. This is a scaled-up prisoner's dilemma: we can't obtain the best overall outcome because no one believes others will cast their lot with the group.

As James Galbraith puts it, "Without public solutions to the problems of life on the treadmill, and without the political parties, platforms and organizations to put them into effect, it is not surprising that people become open to the appeal of every man for himself."[28]

There's no quick fix to this problem, even at the level of addressing it in our messaging. At a minimum, when we're crafting our advocacy for policies to improve public services, we must acknowledge that fears over the quality of our few remaining commons are valid. We tend, justifiably, to go straight to defense (e.g., Medicare users rate it more highly than private insurance; district schools beat charters on the whole). Our accurate rebuttals make it seem we don't understand the impulse many Americans have to go it alone.

This deafness to what real people are feeling drives them toward populist movements that *do* profess to hear them. Enter on cue—the Tea Party. Its solutions may be way off the mark, but its approach—providing a sense of control and agency through shared grievance and narrative—is compelling to a justifiably frightened and disillusioned populace.

In fact, it's deeply ironic that the group championing the further dismantling of any collective institutions chooses the name it has. What's more social than a *party*? Especially the Tea Party, a historic reference that calls to mind individuals acting together in the public square. It employs collective action to undo social institutions. And, arguably, the only way to convince us to do something this destructive to the commons is by dressing it up in the spirit of shared fate, bringing us together in the endeavor. As a social species, humans need connection and interaction.

There's another key thing progressives often fail to provide our listeners: a clear *role* for individuals in our movement and our policy solutions. While it's true and important to emphasize the social and structural: families, communities, states, and even nations are made up of individuals. When we say nothing to individuals, or make no mention of what they need to be doing, their need for direction does not magically disappear. This silence helps fuel many Americans' instinct to go it alone and insist everyone else do the same.

As we'll revisit later on, it's striking how often conservatives directly address their audience—saying a singular or plural "you" and ordering some clear, personal action (work hard, take care of your family, open small businesses). Progressive discourse almost never includes direct address and consistently fails to tell people what they can do right now to be part of the solution.

Individuals need to be heard and feel heard, spoken to plainly, and directed to build something together. Especially in times like these of fierce alienation and terrible uncertainty, we can't convince our fellow Americans to favor strengthening the institutions that bind us without reinforcing how we all belong to, work for, and benefit from these national goods.

The Agency Problem

Roughly speaking, an accurate progressive explanation for inequality proceeds as follows: groups possess differential power, more powerful groups create rules that disadvantage other groups, powerful groups end up better off and thus even more powerful, and disadvantaged groups end up less well off and thus even less powerful.

In order for this causal chain to hold, listeners need to assume that members of any group are endowed with equal abilities, talents, and ambitions. Furthermore, people can make deliberate changes to "the system," in other words, the economy. Therefore, the economy isn't independent; it doesn't have agency.

And with that, we're right back to the metaphor problem we explored in depth earlier. As we saw, the conservative view of the economy is as a self-regulating entity, often likened to a person with ability, authority, and judgment.

In the inequality context, conservatives posit that the economy itself, not the people working in it, generates wealth. Here's one such pearl of wisdom from a *Washington Post* op-ed: "The U.S. economy *hands out wealth* far more evenly."[29] In further support for this favored economic metaphor, former Representative Dick Armey (R-TX) conveys the idea that markets act on their own: "Markets reward successful entrepreneurs and innovations. Just as importantly, however, markets will punish bad ideas and inefficient behavior."[30]

If the market or the economy is presumed to run independently, humans can't possibly rig either. Here, again from Cato's Will Wilkinson, is a statement that clearly exposes our failure to adequately prove that actors and institutions make economic rules and control allocation: "This silly but sadly widespread misimpression [that income is literally distributed] is compounded by talk of the median worker's dwindling 'share' of the 'national income' as if the United States of America was a super-sized firm with profits to be bargained over and divvied up or 'distributed' among the interested parties."[31]

Wilkinson is wrong on the facts, of course. But he's not crazy to cling to this thinking—and he's wise to promote it in service of the further regulatory dismantling he wants to see done. When have we ever pinned the blame for determining distribution with conviction on a person or group?

METAPHORS FOR INEQUALITY

Verbalizing inequality in a credible and coherent way is hard. But some of this is under our control. Just as in the case of talking about the economy as a body, a liquid, or the weather, too much of the time we're letting our words about inequality get in the way of our meaning. Once again, examining the mostly metaphorical models we use to transmit what inequality "is" to our audiences reveals how some of the lack of interest in tackling this issue comes from the imprecision and even contradictions in our language.

Mind the Gap

In the case of inequality, it's most common to characterize the differences between the rich and the poor as though they're objects affixed on opposite sides of a chasm. When people are reasoning about inequality in this way, they use words like "spread": "Incomes rose faster than inflation for most Americans and the spread between rich and poor was much less."[32] Or we can call inequality to mind with expressions like "divide" and "canyon."

By far, the most popular single articulation of this model is "gap," as in the gap between rich and poor or the racial wealth gap. Since we're thinking unconsciously of these differences as separations in space, it's not surprising to hear an expression like closing the gap or, conversely, the widening gap.

Horizontal divide language is popular for good reason. It paints a clear image of what is otherwise intangible and uses something we all experience—physical separation—to convey monetary distance. This model allows us to get vivid and playful with our words. As Arianna Huffington puts it, "The chasm between Americas haves and have nots has reached Grand Canyon-esque proportions."[33]

Not only does such language allow for explanations of current difference, it also offers easy ways to talk about change over time. For example, "Across the political spectrum, there is almost universal acknowledgment that our nation (and planet) are pulling apart economically," or "We will grow together or grow apart."[34]

Further, this language doesn't introduce notions of inherent worth. We can't glean from separation in space that one side is better than another.

But there are irredeemable problems introduced with this language. "Gap" isn't a stirring call to action; it's a clothing store. It may provide a ready image of where we are, but it is static. It says nothing about how we got here. It's all outcome and no cause, all what and no why.

To catalyze desire for change, conveying causation needs to be primary. Again, in the words of economist James Galbraith, "According to popular perception, a high level of inequality is a kind of black rain, a curse of obscure origin with no known remedy, a matter of mystery covered by words like downsizing, deregulation or globalization."[35]

We know the harm in the public not seeing the causes of current conditions: "The staggering loss of wealth in communities of color—financial assets that allow families to weather economic storms and to make investments that enable them and their children to get ahead—*has been allowed to happen as if by accident.*"[36]

Studies of cognition and decades of experience tell us that when we don't provide an explanation, our audiences will fill one in for themselves. In this case, the cause-effect narrative for our gap seems to goes as follows: those who are poor have chosen this condition. Whether it's a character flaw (lazy bum), moral failure (welfare queen), inherent defect (the bell curve), or all of the above, this story tells us what have-nots have not is ambition or intelligence.

As we saw with leading Republicans and their constituents, the tendency is to blame the individual:

> To report that the gap between blacks and whites is due to the legacy of racism, and to ignore the role of marriage, is to polarize further the debate about the role of government in our lives.[37]

> The major underlying factors producing child poverty in the United States are welfare dependence and single parenthood.[38]

If being rich or poor is understood as the result of differential effort, then we can conclude each category is simply a lifestyle choice. Inequality is then a sign that our economy is doing exactly what it should—rewarding the deserving and motivating the lazy. And, the reasoning continues, since there's nothing wrong with this, there's also nothing anybody should do about it.

We use this gap language all the time. And then we wonder why the statistics we cite, the graphs we generate, and the examples we offer of "widening" inequality don't raise the eyebrows, let alone the ire, of our many audiences. Using this language, in effect, tacitly degrades individuals and makes current conditions seem natural. By employing it, we double down on the notion that poverty and riches are the product of individual choice. In reality, that poor people lack income and wealth is in large part the result of the rules financial and political elites crafted to take both of these from them.

A wealth divide further implies we have two separate economies, with the rich on one side and everyone else on the other. The poor even have their own segregated address: the "welfare state." If we believe the wealth of a few has absolutely no relationship to the deprivation of others, than there is no solution for inequality. Because there's no problem.

This is not just a false assumption; it's also a dangerous one. All of us engage with each other, producing, consuming, saving, and investing in our one economy. But the wealthy have stalked off with the lion's share. Yet history shows that all too often some people are unfathomably rich because others are inexcusably poor.

Ultimately, the ability for the wealthy (and reliably white) to see their economic fate as separate from that of their poor countrymen (usually of color) is what facilitates dismantling social supports. Just as literal inequality erodes mutual concern, language that highlights and exacerbates a perception of division does too. With the language of gap and its close correlates, we're actually letting those responsible for the mess we're in off the hook.

The Lofty Heights of Inequality

As we've seen, inequality can be represented horizontally; it also makes sense to talk of it as a vertical difference. "Top" and "bottom"—for example, "They and their successors fought hard to lift up the bottom and bring down the top"[39]—are the most popular words we use to indicate we're doing just this. But there are other expressions that trigger this way of thinking:

a more *hierarchical* society[40]

the *summits* of Corporate America[41]

plunge them into such *deep* financial and emotional straits[42]

This model helps our old linguistic nemesis "trickle-down economics" function. After all, in order for something to descend from above, we must imagine this particular component of the economy—money—as residing in the vertical plane. It also helps lend coherence to notions of "bottom-up" economic growth and the "income pyramid."

Most progressives writing about inequality are far less likely to use this kind of language—gap is the more relied-upon model—but it too appears from time to time:

In spite of the odds, women of color are energetic and entrepreneurial in their efforts to gain a toehold on the economic ladder.[43]

many households at the *lowest positions* on the wealth distribution[44]

A few at the very *top* ran away with nearly all of the gains.[45]

The draw of this model is clear. Unlike the previous one, it emerges from and reinforces the idea of shared fate. You can't have something above another element unless they are in some contact. People are on top *because* others are below. This language also implies the economy as a single container: "There is a giant hole at the bottom of the American economy that has been engulfing poor families for decades."[46] We are all *in* this together.

Another boon of verticality is that it is easy to visualize—all of us have put one thing on top of another. It also provides us tangible terms for numerating problems; in this metaphor that could sound like *people getting stepped on* or *inequality crushing those least well off.*

But there's a reason the vertical metaphor is the unchallenged favorite way conservatives describe this issue (when they deign to broach the topic at all, that is). This is because it introduces hierarchy (literally) and with it a sense of superiority and deservedness. George Lakoff illustrated this thinking by pointing out how, as a vice presidential candidate, Dan Quayle questioned our graduated income tax by asking, "Why should the best people be punished?"[47]

In English, we routinely understand good as up and bad as down. We can hear this in phrases like *He was down in the dumps* and *Things are looking up*. When we call the wealthy "the top," we're powerfully conveying they are better than everyone else. So, it follows, the poor, as "the bottom," are worse.

Consider our tendency to talk about what someone is "worth." While this may literally be a question of their net earnings or wealth, it suggests moral superiority. Examine, for illustration, this one-word slip of a reporter's tongue describing an African American woman who overcame great odds to send her daughter to an exclusive college: "Williams was poor but smart."[48] Not poor *and* smart, the word "but" practically shouts the belief that these traits don't belong together.

John Galt, Ayn Rand's protagonist in *Atlas Shrugged*, expressed elitism in vertical language perfectly: "The man at the top of the intellectual pyramid contributes the most to all those below him, but gets nothing except his material payment, receiving no intellectual bonus from others to add to the value of his time. The man at the bottom who, left to himself, would starve in his hopeless ineptitude, contributes nothing to those above him, but receives the bonus of all of their brains."[49] Rand serves, of course, as philosopher-queen to conservative leaders from Paul Ryan to Glenn Beck and Ron Paul to Clarence Thomas. In fact, Rand's biographer Jennifer Burns calls the author "the ultimate gateway drug to life on the right."[50]

It's no wonder we pull ourselves "up" (not forward or along) by our bootstraps. This model helps suggest why people are in their relative positions. Our most basic assumptions about ladders are that you should use them to get higher. When we introduce this metaphor, we imply that people's lack of wealth is of their own making.

This, as before, is a hazard of zeroing in on outcomes without specifying what caused them. When we stick merely to describing how things are and leave open the question of how they came to be, we're leaving room for folks who benefit greatly from inequality to narrate why it exists.

Equally Unhelpful Ways to Think About Inequality

While separation in space, whether vertical or horizontal, get most of the airtime, there are still other ways to think of this topic. Before turning, finally, to more promising metaphors I'd have us employ, let's briefly touch upon two other models in play.

Inequality can be thought of as imbalance. Imagine a scale—when one side goes up, the other goes down. Because this shares basic components with the vertical model, we see some of the same language. For instance, "Our *top-heavy* era has evolved from a heavily bankrolled effort by conservatives and corporations."[51] But it's the reference to weight that tips us off that imbalance is key. This is where playing field comes in, with reference to the need to have it be "level." In President Obama's 2009 budget proposal, we see this commentary: "There is something wrong when we allow the *playing field to be tilted* so far in the favor of so few."[52]

Like the vertical model with which it shares elements, this model does much in the way of profiling interconnection. It's hard to imagine a more direct way to convey that when something happens in one place, it directly affects another. Here someone describes just such a process—when weight is removed from one end, it helps lighten the load: "Fairer policies would share the risks of our entrepreneurial economy by helping *balance* the economic burdens among all of us, rather than *piling them onto* people of color, the poor."[53]

But this benefit is also a major pitfall. As with any fulcrum, by using this metaphor, we're telling our audiences, when one side rises, the other falls. Your loss is my gain. When we reduce inequality to two sides vying directly against each other, it triggers zero-sum thinking. This comes through loud and clear to conservatives, and they react strongly against it. As P. J. O'Rourke puts it, "The notion of economic equality is based on an ancient and ugly falsehood central to bad economic thinking: There's a fixed amount of wealth."[54]

In reality, life is far more complex than a seesaw could ever describe. While this is true of all the models (otherwise they wouldn't be simplifications), the particular set of ideas prompted here are so reductionist, the audience can't hear much else. Once we trigger this 'what's bad for you is good for me' thinking, those on "top" are yet more determined to stop any attempt to alter the status quo.

Finally, one last model before we get to the good stuff. It's an understatement to say that progressives are actively opposed to extreme inequality. The problem looms large in our work, so it can be tempting to call it like it is and describe inequality as a powerful force or even, more specifically, as an opponent. And we do.

Inequality is guilty of many things. Avowedly progressive Fox News contributor Sally Kohn charges, for example, "The middle class is rapidly joining the ranks of the poor, reeling from the inevitable, *gravitational, polarizing pull of inequity*."[55]

So powerful is inequality that we speak of combating it. We must "confront directly the threat posed by this inequality."[56] And we're not the only ones facing this foe: "The bill that President Obama signed on Tuesday is the federal government's *biggest attack* on economic inequality since inequality began rising more than three decades ago."[57]

Here's the problem with this language: inequality is not a self-propelled force. It's largely a human creation. While it's great to offer up such powerful terms for just how bad inequality is and the harms that it causes, by imbuing inequality with agency and intentionality, we help others think of it as like a tornado or an earthquake. Natural disasters are horrible things, and we do expect government to step in with emergency funds and assistance, but we know people aren't to blame for the destruction. This false parallel makes it, once again, hard to see the causes of inequality.

Just as imbuing "the market" with agency cripples debate about the correct role of government, speaking of inequality as an independent, powerful actor makes it very hard to come back to a conversation about what can and should be done. After all, if inequality is evil unleashed, mere policies won't stop it. We need to insist with our language that people made this mess and they can and must fix it.

TOWARD AN EFFECTIVE INEQUALITY DISCOURSE

So how do we get the word out about economic inequality? Not just how much of it exists, but also where it comes from and why it's destroying the long-term stability of American society and the proper functioning of our economy?

Inequality as Internal Imbalance

A welcome contrast to language that gives agency to inequality itself by portraying it as a force or an opponent, and thus denying people agency by failing to mention them, is the progressive notion of inequality as instability in the economic system.

Being off balance is a familiar and unpleasant experience that transcends demographic groups. No matter where you're from or what you have, you've spun yourself into dizziness at one time or another. What this model refers to is an instability that can only be righted internally. Examples of language that evoke this include "out of balance" and an economy that has "gotten off kilter."

Admittedly, the potential for confusing this model with the scale language criticized before is great. The important distinction is the careful avoidance of two, and exactly two, actors compared in movement or position.

Though not currently in wide use, this model offers much to recommend it. Besides assuming interdependence, it avoids hierarchical notions of superiority and simplistic reductions to winners and losers. Further, it fits in conceptually with the idea of the economy as an object in motion. As entities move through space, putting undue weight on one side skews their intended trajectory. A car weighted down in the back will scrape along the road; an unbalanced plane will not keep its course. This is precisely what's evoked with language like "off kilter."

This language is most applicable for discussing the effects inequality has on the overall economy. It helps us explain why vast differences are bad for all of us and for the economic system we operate in together.

Inequality as a Barrier

Having a positive way to explain why inequality harms the whole nation is key. But we also need a way to describe how inequality affects individuals and groups. Instead of a "gap between rich and poor," we're far better served calling it a "barrier."

A barrier connotes a big, imposing wall behind which a few can hoard the goodies, while those on the other side are left wanting. When you barricade yourself in, you keep others out. Instead of asking to "bridge the divide," we should insist on dismantling the obstacles that keep too many from the gains that have come from their own hard work.

Before delving into details of how and why we should consider this language, I return us to the commonplace metaphor upon which this model relies: life as a journey. We saw this earlier in discussing the promising explanation for the economy's purpose: to facilitate people's journeys through life. Having this explanation emerge here again only underscores how well the suggested models for the economy fit tightly together with what I'm arguing makes sense to say about inequality.

Again, there are hundreds of mundane ways this metaphor enters our vocabulary. If we're *rushing into something*, our friends may urge us to *put the brakes on* and think for a bit. Conversely, they may tell us to *get this show on the road* and decide already.

Life as a journey is a ubiquitous metaphor, and so it's not surprising to find it in talk about the economy. Beyond the examples explored before, we see talk of an "income starting line."[58] A progressive author asks, "Why [are] so many young adults . . . finding it so hard to get ahead[?]"[59]

Life can be construed as a journey, steps taken from a start-ing point to a destination. Something that hinders this trajec-tory is commonly called a barrier; this, in economic space, is what inequality does to individuals. As we also saw, we can reason about the economy as a means to facilitate our life's travels. This allows us to invert the unhelpful authority the economy currently wields over us by putting it in its place as something that should make our lives better and easier.

In fact, we see the vehicle metaphor used directly to ex-plain why we should address inequality: "Trying to revive *our stalled and stumbling economy* without addressing the funda-mental problem of inequality that got us here is like trying to fix the flat tire on your car just by adding air. It's no solution at all: there's still a hole in your tire."[60]

Admittedly, the barrier metaphor is not much used in writ-ten language about inequality. But, again, my conversations with leading progressive economic thinkers revealed them using it time and again. Crafting our narrative from this metaphor, we would say something like the following: "In-equality holds people back from contributing to our nation. It sets in place obstacles not only to success but also to survival. Trapping some Americans in poverty, policies that promote in-equality exclude certain groups from making a living no matter how much they work. The rules we've crafted block access to resources and opportunities and prevent huge numbers of us from participating meaningfully in our economy."

It's absolutely true, as conservatives boast, material condi-tions are far better today than decades ago, and America's poor often have what seem like riches to the rest of the world. But we know from extensive psychological study that even relative privation causes irreparable harm. Namely, a sense of feeling trapped. Knowing you are capable of more and seeing other people easily obtain it are what make unequal societies so hard to take. Conservatives deride this as envy, but seeing someone flourish where you struggle to survive is its own harm.

A key word here is "access"; that's what a barrier denies people. For example, "access to opportunities," "access to wealth," and "equal access to resources." Access means you are no longer bound. This affords individuals the freedom to give their talents to the national economy and the nation, in turn, to benefit from what every individual offers. The more we have everyone participating fully in the economy, the more effectively the whole system functions.

The metaphor of inequality as a barrier, wall, or other obstruction highlights several critical truths about our economy. These objects are human-made. This conveys that inequality is not some God-given, inevitable, natural wonder. We have built these barriers, and we can bring them down. In other words, there's another way our economy can be structured if we elect and work for it.

This model serves as a powerful critique of the vertical one. There the expectation is that given a ladder, you should pull yourself up. The focus here is not on the outcome but on the process. Thus, it also addresses the main problem of the gap language: it answers the question of why things are how they are. Impediments block anyone regardless of efforts or abilities.

Conservatives see obstacles created by government intrusion: "We have the right to achieve whatever our ambition and talents allow, with no one permitted to *forcibly stop us* " and "Government handouts . . . *trap the poor* in a vicious cycle of dependency."[61] In contrast, we see barriers constructed from the unjust rules that concentrate power in too few hands. Regardless, we all share distaste for constraints.

This points to another promising aspect of this approach: it's widely accessible and based in lived experience. From benign inconveniences like being stuck in traffic to horrifying ordeals like living behind prison walls, we know that things outside ourselves impede us.

These barriers go against deeply American notions of freedom in its broadest sense and folk traditions more specifically about unfettered movement. "Go west" and "The tough get going" are deeply ingrained in our nation's psyche. "Don't fence me in" is the poetry of the cowboy, but it also resonates strongly with the entrepreneur. Not to mention those NASCAR fans we're always trying to bring to our cause.

Inequality as barrier centers attention on process; it makes a credible case that's not about lack of effort or intelligence for why certain groups can't catch up with others. It lets us have our language lay the blame where it belongs: on the obstructions erected by decades of greed and concentrated wealth and power, not on the people who find themselves trapped on the wrong side of them.

RECOGNIZING WHAT WE CAN CHANGE

Returning for a moment to Norton and Ariely's study on how ordinary Americans perceive inequality, I am most struck by the assumptions they enforced in their approach. In asking people what level of inequality they favored, the psychologists instantly implied that this is something we can select. In other words, how much wealth is in how few hands is no accident. It's a matter of law, policy, and practice.

Sadly, we almost never speak from this accurate position. Instead, we allow the 1%, who benefit royally from keeping the rules as they are, to define the terms of this debate. Accepting language that suggests inequality is natural and of unknown origins, not to mention parroting notions that wealth equals worth, we make it difficult for our problem diagnoses to make sense. Never mind our suggested policy solutions.

As john a. powell says, "Choosing an approach to poverty is mainly motivated by how one sees the targeted group on *the gradient of belonging*."[62] This is what the language of barrier enables for us. It tells us some are purposefully kept out, while others move themselves into communities of security-guarded prosperity.

Rereading the speeches of Dr. Martin Luther King Jr., I noticed something striking. Although he talks about inequality in almost every sentence, he never mentions "gaps" or uses words like "top" and "bottom." His is in fact the language of barriers—obstacles constructed with the express purpose of keeping people out: "One hundred years later, the Negro lives on *a lonely island of poverty in the midst of a vast ocean of material prosperity*. One hundred years later, the Negro is still *languished in the corners* of American society and finds himself *an exile in his own land*."[63]

Of course, in a time of segregation this language made literal sense. But it holds true even today. For two people to sit at the same lunch counter, they have to be able to afford the same meal. Barriers are very much still in place, and they, not lack of will, ability, or deservedness, are separating us and distorting our society.

CHAPTER 5

Words Mean Things

---

*We have now sunk to a depth at which the restatement
of the obvious is the first duty of intelligent men.*
—GEORGE ORWELL, *ADELPHI*

In 2008, psychologist Christopher Bryan and his research
team at Stanford University made a startling discovery:
people's voting behavior could hinge on a word. Surveying registered Californians, they asked half the respondents whether
they'd vote and the other half what seems like the same thing,
only phrased a bit differently. In the second group, they asked
each person if he or she intended to "be a voter."

The difference was stunning. Where just over 50 percent
of the people asked about voting said that they intended to do
so, 87.5 percent of respondents questioned about being a
voter signaled a desire to get to the polls. And this difference
went far beyond just what people said they would do. Post-
election voting records showed 96 percent of those surveyed
about being a voter actually went and pulled the lever.[1]

Considering Americans' famous reluctance to get to the polls, this difference is all the more striking. Where campaigns spend generously to get out the vote, here we see a wording difference accomplishing what calling, carpooling, and cajoling often fail to make happen.

But these two questions—"Will you vote?" versus "Will you be a voter?"—offer up far more than a simple word difference. These two formulations represent a conceptual shift from action to identity, from what you do to who you are.

Americans think of a voter as a generally good and responsible person. People want to see themselves as voters. Nonetheless, even among those who bother to register, not all of them actually carry out the activity that would earn them this label.

Bryan's study reveals that simply taking on this identity, or more accurately voicing the intention to do so in an interview, bolsters the respondent's attachment to carrying out the action. It's one thing to say we're going to do something and then not do it. It's quite another to adopt a positive identity and then have to give it up.

We've seen that metaphors can shape what's true for our audiences. They can also determine what the public feels like doing and how we come to judgments about what ought to be done. This same power holds true for other linguistic forms.

When we take care to select words that affirm what we believe, we increase the odds our audiences will understand and trust us. If the stars align, they may even take up our cause. Unfortunately, right now we too readily imply ideas at odds with our intentions. At best this makes us sound incoherent; at worst we seem opportunistic or entirely unsure what we actually want to achieve.

As I'll explain, progressive advocates' love affair with the passive voice—not naming a person in the subject position of our sentences—has hindered our ability to portray why things are the way they are. And, with it, how things could be different and better. Next, I will explore how we characterize the key players in our economic drama: the wealthy, the poor, and the middle class.

PEOPLE DO THINGS

Right now, in the economic realm and beyond, our words convey the message that policies magically change, bad things come to pass, and problems are mysteriously visited upon us. Take, for example, the economic expressions we've grown so accustomed to hearing that we take them for granted. "The unemployment rate rose" and "The dollar fell" suggest that these figures are self-propelled. This belies the human actions (or failure to act) lying behind observed outcomes.

Unsurprisingly, there are real decisions behind changes in our economy. Economists like Dean Baker have credibly demonstrated how right-to-work laws now in twenty-two states, outsource-promoting trade agreements, and even patent and copyright rules all have a hand in driving down the number of person-hours available to U.S. workers. Similarly, monetary policy to control inflation, in place since the Volcker years, ensured the relative value of the dollar would favor imports, thus propelling the U.S. trade deficits with, among other places, China.[2]

And yet we insist on implying things simply occur. The polite passive voice we've adopted may make us sound reasoned and neutral—like coolheaded experts or academics. But it obscures the truth and lets guilty parties off the hook.

When we learned, for example, that former New Jersey governor Jon Corzine was involved in shady financial dealings, the *New York Times* reported this by saying, "Regulators have discovered that hundreds of millions of dollars in customer money *have gone missing* from MF Global, the brokerage firm run by Jon S. Corzine."[3] I don't pretend to know the details of goings-on at MF Global, but I can assure you, dollars did not sprout wings and fly.

We tend also to speak this way about wages. Economist John Schmitt says, for example, "Wages . . . have *trailed far behind* growth in productivity over the last thirty years, and, for many groups of workers, wages *have actually stagnated or even fallen* in inflation-adjusted terms."[4] This suggests wages are capable of locomotion.

Of course, no one believes that these things are literally true. Even so, the way we frame our messages primes audiences to unconsciously *get* certain concepts while obscuring others. In talking about wages as self-propelled, we miss out on the chance to highlight the external pressures—the actors—causing compensation levels to change.

Frame, used here in the linguistic sense, simply signals that words occur in set contexts. We bring to everything we see and hear our prior experiences with and embedded assumptions about how the world works. Take, for example, the competing possible characterizations of someone who is loathe to spend money. Some of us would call such a person "thrifty," while others would apply the term "stingy."

Arguably, these are descriptors for the same behavior, but they bring with them vastly different beliefs about how money ought to be spent—or, depending on your vantage point, saved. By selecting between "cheap" and "prudent," to offer a couple of synonyms, we also insert our judgment about how people ought to behave.

In considering just how we frame our talk about wages, we would do better to talk about them as returns to workers for the value they've created. Wages are a share of the profits workers generate. Thus, describing their movement should include references to people. Rewriting the above, we could say, "Over the last thirty years business has given workers less and less of the wealth they created," or "Over the last thirty years CEOs have confiscated and hoarded more and more of the wealth their workers created."

Sadly, versions of this passive voice, "mistakes were made" rhetoric is a staple in the economic realm. It's a meaningless collection of words sometimes masquerading as milquetoast apology. No one actually has to admit anything deliberate went wrong. Is it any wonder, as mentioned earlier, that we have yet to see a single CEO held liable for the double-dealing, evasion, and outright fraud that inflated the housing bubble until it burst into full-fledged recession?

Even our orator president, in another part of his speech in Osawatomie, Kansas, showed off his ability to hold no one accountable: "For most Americans, the basic bargain that made this country great *has eroded.* Long before the recession hit, *hard work stopped paying off* for too many people. . . . [Most people] struggled with *costs that were growing and paychecks that weren't*—and too many *families found themselves racking up more and more debt* just to keep up" (emphasis added).

As mentioned before, the Obama team selected this date and location to echo Theodore Roosevelt's populist call for a "new nationalism." The *Los Angeles Times*, *Boston Globe*, and liberal super-blog Daily Kos all heralded the speech. They called it a long-awaited shift in Obama from conciliatory non-combatant to champion of the people. Yet seeing the passive voice run rampant here in particular highlights just how far we're off the mark.

Costs for basic necessities did not grow like some freaky tumor. Similarly, paychecks didn't inexplicably shrink relative to those aforementioned expenses. These are the results of at least three decades worth of real work by CEOs, conservative politicians, and lobbyists to dismantle labor unions, roll back health care coverage and pensions, and suppress real wages even as profits and executive bonuses soared. These people worked hard to screw most of us, and they've been wildly successful at this mission. Let's give credit where due.

As the most quotable example, I offer up AIG's CEO Maurice "Hank" Greenberg. When a whistleblowing employee confided to a firm lawyer that AIG was cheating state governments out of tens of millions of dollars by cooking the books on workers compensation premiums, it became clear that Greenberg knew what had been happening all along. He then famously quipped, "All I want in life is an unfair advantage." And he made sure to have one, by every means legal and not he could invent.[5]

Our failure to put humans in the subject position of our sentences creates problems beyond recognizing and punishing bad actors. When we convey that faceless forces (or invisible hands) are behind good and bad outcomes, we send the message we can't do anything about anything. No wonder people believe government can't improve conditions and we must accept whatever fate the economy hands us. We've implied time and again this is the case.

And it isn't just supposedly neutral newspaper writers or avowed conservatives who are doing it. Groups Fox News likes to call communist fronts, such as Occupy Wall Street, National People's Action, and Center for Community Change, in their crusade for principal reductions on mortgages rely upon phrases like "People lost their homes." Even I, who lose my keys on a weekly basis, have never managed to misplace my house. People do not lose their homes. Lenders seize them—evicting grandmothers and forcing fathers to tell school kids their rooms are no longer their own.

We use the passive voice at our peril. It is not only bad writing; it also hardens our hearts to the plight of the worst off. As we saw in discussing inequality, if we do not embed what causes some to want for nothing while others have nothing but want, we cannot effectively argue for policies that will shift this reality.

Nor is it just in the description of the problem that we rely upon passive constructions. Progressive calls for solutions are similarly de-peopled:

> Occupational segregation, wage disparities, and the lack of fringe benefits tied to the "wealth escalator" (e.g. 401(k)s, health insurance, paid sick days) *must be addressed*.[6]

Reforms are needed to ensure that such opportunities and rewards are distributed equitably.[7]

The Bush era tax cuts *being considered need to be analyzed*.[8]

Policymakers likely feel relieved and thrilled by these statements. They can easily agree without having to do anything. The "asks" don't even involve direct asking.

Conservative activists could give us lessons on making effective demands. They are on the record as wanting a flat tax, privatization of Social Security, vouchers for schools, and public funding for churches. Their requests are clear, sustained, and deliberate. In fact, arguably the most visible and successful longtime conservative prodder, Grover Norquist, actually has senators, representatives, and other elected officials sign a pledge never to raise taxes in any circumstances. You don't catch activists on the right hedging like progressives inevitably do.

Further, not calling for accountability and not naming names also facilitate our disconnection from those in positions of power. "The Treasury," for example, helps determine who among us keeps our paychecks and at what wages. Buying and selling dollars, Treasury sets the value of our currency and with it determines whether it's even cheaper to get stuff from China or makes economic sense to buy Made in the U.S.A. The seemingly mundane business of printing money is actually how choices are made about the amount of manufacturing we will still do here. Aren't you tempted to pull back the curtain to see the people who are pulling these strings?

When we fail to see government as made up of people, it's harder to hold those in power accountable. On the flip side, it also blinds us from any notion that our elected and appointed public servants do, sometimes, serve the public. When "the Department of Education decides" or "the White House declares," it's easy enough to forget real people work in these places.

Consider the portion of our government that consistently receives positive reviews; it's also one of the few whose members are named as people. I'm speaking, of course, of the military or—more aptly—"our brave men and women in arms."

Granted, the esteem we have—even though only platitudes and broken promises—for our military is due to far more than good PR. Nonetheless, when we contrast overall public opinion of "our troops" with the vile rhetoric spewed about the members of public sector unions, elected leaders, and administration officials at every level of government, the difference is striking.

Van Jones often remarks that he's never met a "public sector worker." Neither have I. The people we know are teachers, firefighters, public health nurses, and police officers. By calling them what they really are, Jones is conveying something the spokespeople for the armed forces intuitively grasp: it's much easier to vilify a category than it is to generate distaste for actual people.

We too readily turn our government institutions into faceless bureaucracies run without humans. It's a short hop from there to nodding along when tax-avenger Norquist declares that if he could, he would "drown government in a bath tub."[9]

If we thought about government as the people in our neighborhood, we would be outraged to hear his intention to set off on a killing spree. Further, if we had any sense of government as "we the people," we'd realize he means to eliminate *us*.

But who cares about a collection of buildings? Who will fight for the rights of endless "departments" or myriad "task forces"? Is it any wonder people don't like members of Congress even when they report liking their own representative?

To paraphrase Ellen Bravo of 9 to 5, "people say women earn less than men because they don't ask for more money. Women earn less than men because men pay them less. People do things—if we don't convey this, there's little hope anything else we say will have meaning or impact.

BRINGING THE AUDIENCE IN ON THE ACTION

Embracing what I'm calling the people do things approach to communication about the economy extends well beyond describing the actions of elites and electeds. There are additional gains to be made, in terms of the accuracy and impact of our messages, by speaking directly to and involving our audiences.

"Do you pay too much for your auto insurance?" "Your place for low prices." "What you've been looking for . . . " Sound familiar? The most popular word in advertising is "you"; it even has "free" and "new" beat.[10] Unfortunately, message makers on the left haven't caught onto this. The right and the private sector, knowing much better, score big by speaking to and bringing their audiences in on the action.

Ronald Reagan, in his 1964 "A Time for Change" speech, used "you and I" no less than ten times. Many conservatives hail these remarks as seminal, the speech that made his presidency possible.[11] Reagan connected with Americans; in characterizing response to increased government assistance, he cleverly presupposed the public was skeptical, saying, "Anytime *you and I question the schemes of the do-gooders*, we're denounced as being opposed to their humanitarian goals." He elevated us by continuing, "You and I have the courage to say to our enemies 'there is a price we will not pay.'" And he even made the Barry Goldwater election about American identity, declaring, "You and I have a rendezvous with destiny." The Gipper—he's just one of us!

The right seems to come naturally to this language. To judge from the speeches of conservatives, their approach seems to hinge on adding things to our to-do lists. The first thing they'd assign to us is to work hard. Somewhere in there we're supposed to haul up on our bootstraps, wed someone of the opposite sex, reproduce, buy stuff, and raise kids. If we have spare time, we should protest abortion clinics, go to church, and buy guns. All of these implied commands or direct instructions bring the public in on the action.

Theirs is the mantra of personal responsibility. Their public appeals are all about what you can and should do in your life. They do this with no apparent irony: the party of get-government-out is much more likely to tell you how to live your life, going so far as to dictate appropriate romantic attachments and family structures. Deciding for you what it's ok to feel, even more generally, falls under their domain. If, for example, you are bothered by observed inequities in our society, you're told to curtail your unwarranted (and unholy) envy, as we saw earlier.

Direct address ("you") tells us that these politicians are talking to us. It's you, not just someone else, who will be affected. They're coming to take *your* money, *your* freedom, give condoms to *your* kindergartner, and stop *you* from celebrating Christmas. As Gerald Ford said, in a quotation often misattributed to Barry Goldwater, at his fear-mongering best, "A government big enough to give you everything you want is a government big enough to take from you everything you have."[12]

They also have the nauseating tendency to address us as friends. John McCain loved this moniker, once referring to "my friends" twenty-four times in a single ninety-minute campaign appearance.[13] Mitt Romney likely forgot about YouTube when he countered a question at a rally with an off-the-cuff "Corporations are people, my friends."[14] Yeah, pal, you said it.

Considering what they actually stand for, their constant use of "you" in all permutations is vile. They're dedicated to keeping most of us out of the clique they've created. In fact, this is a textbook example of protesting too much. The only thing most of us are let in on is their cheap talk; the policies they favor are not for you and me.

Progressives, in contrast, actually mean "you" in the southern pluralized sense of the word. We even mean "them." The rights that we fight for are intended to benefit the many—even those who oppose us at every turn.

Yet it's been a long time since John F. Kennedy instructed us to "ask not what your country can do for you, ask what you can do for your country." Likely this has become a commence-ment speech standby precisely because we're so unaccus-tomed to having politicians on the left speak directly to their audiences. Much less ask something of them. We're much more likely to hear Democrats of all persuasions, progressives among them, speak in vague generalities about what has hap-pened and what's to come.

I'm not entirely sure why we've cut "you" and permutations of it from our public vocabulary. Perhaps progressives have done too many workshops in nonviolent communication and become schooled in making "I" statements. Perhaps the omis-sion is gendered—where masculine-dominated cultures like the Republican Party go to issuing orders, balanced or femi-nine ones favor airing grievances, opening up possibilities, and not imposing their views.

Whatever the impetus, we need to cut it out. Progressives' public statements often make us sound too much like aca-demics and too seldom like regular people. Further, as we're generally fighting about and for issues of fairness, security, livelihood, and well-being for all, we're long overdue in con-veying to audiences that we're talking to you.

CASTING THE CHARACTERS

If we're to come around to ditching abstraction and re-peopling our political rhetoric, we must reexamine how we characterize some of the lead players in our economic show. Discussions of the economy don't go on long without mention of "the wealthy." Once again, we can credit Occupy Wall

Street for making this even more prevalent today. By design, conservatives and progressives have differing opinions on the rich, which inform and propel our divergent views on what inequality is and whether it's a problem.

We've trapped ourselves in a conceptual muddle by implying the wealthy produce national good. Just moments after defending himself against allegations of stirring up class warfare by insisting that no one envies the rich, President Obama said in his 2012 State of the Union, "We're going to push hard to make sure someone making over a million dollars a year aren't [sic] getting tax breaks and tax subsidies they don't need."

We may think "make money" is a neutral expression, a way of saying receive a certain amount. But we don't use "make" to describe riches from inheritance or lottery winnings. It's supposed to convey remuneration for efforts. With this in mind, note that we do use it for gains from investments, as in "I made money off the market this year."

This far-from-benign phrase suggests that the rich manufacture wealth. When, in fact, wealth comes from our resources and our labor acting upon them. Just ask Adam Smith.

In our consumer-driven economy especially, additional money circulates into the system when the poor and middle class are allowed more dollars to spend. The notion that the rich fabricate wealth out of nothing is not only false; it also lends credence to the fantasy those with more money are inherently better than us.

This serves as the backdrop for spinning stories about "job creators." And with it, justification for preserving our millionaire charity spree and taxing capital gains at rates far below those for earned income. We want people to get that money is money. If anything, what comes via sweat is more rightly for keeps than the ticker tape riches handed out from investments.

The idea that money is "made" by the rich fits beautifully in a conservative worldview. Harvard economics professor Kenneth Rogoff asserts, "Many super-earners are also super-creative and bring enormous value."[15] A sentiment echoed by many others:

> The poor hold guaranteed entitlements on $7 trillion of un-funded tax liabilities, for their old age and health benefits, which can only be paid for by the rich, who are the nation's producers.[16]

> There is no fixed, pre-existing glob of income that somehow oozes disproportionately into the pockets of the rich. Wealth is *created*. The top fifth of the population have ten times more income than the bottom fifth because they have *pro-duced* ten times more.[17]

In fact, to hear conservatives tell it, not only do the rich do our producing; they're also good Samaritans:

> Using the wealthy to pull the rest of us along is a very effective redistribution mechanism. No government-sponsored welfare system could deliver anywhere near the benefits that free markets routinely confer on American consumers.[18]

Inequality of wealth and income . . . is the implement that
makes the consumers supreme in giving them the power to
force all those engaged in production to comply with their
orders. . . . He who best serves the consumers profits most
and accumulates riches.[19]

Top-performing CEOs in corporate America earn every
penny of their compensation and then some. They create
wealth, and by doing so create shareholder value, increased
consumer welfare and higher standards of living.[20]

Referring to the wealthy as creators of social good is a conservative framework that not only accepts but also applauds
rampant inequality. The fact is, the rich don't produce or
"make" money; they seize it. To get that point across, we need
to steer clear of this dangerous phrase.

On the flip side, the ways we characterize the poor too
often demote them. You'd think living below the poverty line
in a society with ever-fewer social supports was bad enough.
Heap upon this our tendency to speak of the poor as a class
of people who cannot do for themselves.

Progressive language often suggests helplessness in an
earnest attempt to direct attention, support, and resources to
the poor. For example, "This is an unmitigated disaster for real
people trying to hold their lives together," and "This life of
debt serfdom often begins in college."[21] Underwater, strug-
gling to keep it together, under master's control—the poor
have no agency. We're conveying there is something about
them that can't succeed.

Surely, this isn't our intent, but in speaking about life in poverty in such disempowering terms, we then face a challenge in portraying the poor as creating value and being fully in charge of their lives.

The poor are also frequently portrayed by progressives as prey—as in the common phrase "predatory lending." Or victims of various kinds:

African Americans and Latinos were the *disproportionate targets* for the unfair, deceptive and reckless lending practices that triggered the foreclosure collapse and imploded the credit markets.[22]

When *economically stressed and frightened people are anxious and sullen*, you never know who will capture their fears and hopes.[23]

With little or no access to this essential protection, *these communities are nearly defenseless against the economic disasters* recklessly caused by wealthy individuals and corporations.[24]

These well-intentioned efforts to evoke the plight of the poor have a role, but there's very little counterweight to them. We need more said about the possibilities the poor present for enriching our nation. The poor work hard. Where's the credit for all they do?

Balancing our desire to illustrate what the poor face while honoring their abilities is no small feat. Right now, there are no perfect answers. In the meantime, one thing we must fix is the complete silence of the poor themselves. Every construction is about "them." Not only does this smack of paternalism and lead us to craft policy on behalf of a constituency that may not favor it; it also implies a very dangerous thing.

If the poor are capable and knowledgeable about what needs to happen to them—and we claim they are—why don't we see them speak for themselves? This makes audiences think they don't care, haven't formulated opinions, or can't communicate. Hardly characteristics for a group of people we insist contributes and stands poised to give more if we stop oppressing them.

In fact, we display a tendency to suggest the economic problems of the poor, especially people of color, simply come out of the ether. There are bad outcomes that simply happen.

We're so loathe to name villains, it's as if we've forgotten how. The few times we get close, we can't seal the deal. Note how these advocates for addressing racial wealth disparities suggest current conditions are caused by something concrete but still don't tell us exactly who did it:

> Their ability to build wealth *has been negatively impacted by the cumulative effect of historical policies* restricting people of color and women from asset building opportunities, and by current policies and practices that continue to exacerbate those gaps.[25]

> For racial and ethnic minority women, lack of retirement preparation *can be attributed to* lower wages earned over a lifetime compared to other groups, *occupational segmenta-*

tion, and unequal access to wealth builders such as pensions and employer-sponsored retirement plans.[26]

While these examples suggest something deliberate is behind bad results, what we don't hear is that certain people are to blame. Without naming villains, we cannot expect our audiences to see the harm as intentional—not accidental or anecdotal. Unless we show that people did bad things, it's impossible to believe people could do other things that would lead to desirable new outcomes. The greatest danger in not clarifying someone intentionally did something bad to someone else and must be made to fix it immediately is skirting dangerously close to suggesting individuals bear culpability for their conditions.

Given the human tendency to embrace simple causation and to have trouble seeing complex systems at work, it's very easy to have our words suggest victims are behind what's being done deliberately to them. Notice how these sentences by progressives about racial wealth disparity can easily be read as written by conservatives eager to blame people for what befalls them:

children of color lagging behind their white and Asian peers[27]

Some decades after the victories of the Civil Rights movement, *people of color have not achieved* economic equality, and *are, in fact, slipping backward* in the current downturn.[28]

The nation cannot continue to lead if its fastest growing populations *fail to access* the opportunities associated with gaining middle class status.[29]

While I have no doubts about what these authors *mean* to convey, their language repeatedly implies that individuals are culpable. When we say, "71% of black children live in low-income households and more than 40% live in households with neither savings nor investments,"[30] we likely trigger listeners to think, "Those lazy spendthrifts!" That's why establishing a source of harm is so crucial.

Compare this with the other side's all-too-eager embrace of good guys and bad. The Axis of Evil isn't just about foreigners anymore. Conservatives have no trouble calling out "government bureaucrats," "welfare queens," and "public sector workers" and blaming them for all of our troubles.

It's an open question how to best characterize the rich and the poor. But Occupy Wall Street taught us one thing: the needs and interests of the poor must be aligned with those of the middle class. Allowing any wedge between them weakens the progressive case.

But what about the middle class? Those "working people," "everyday Americans," and "regular folks" politicians love to mention. To hear us tell it, the middle class "grows," "shrinks," "is crumbling," "is joining the ranks of the poor," "is squeezed," and "erodes." But this is about how the middle class gets affected from the outside. There's almost nothing about what the middle class *is*.

Is it, for example, an immutable characteristic—a way of being in the world, as we describe the poor? Or is it more a lifestyle—a set of things owned and accomplished, like the rich? This notable lack of discourse on, to coin a phrase, *middle-classness* is a lost opportunity. We should be able to assign descriptors to the middle class that convey it's a desirable place we should want to be.

Consider the polls that tell us, year after year, around 90 percent of Americans believe themselves to be middle class.[31] We could take a lesson from Pixar's movie *The Incredibles*. When his mother declares everyone is special, the young boy in the film retorts that just means that no one is. Our national insistence that we're all middle class more aptly conveys there's really not much meaning to this designation.

We've seen a shift in our culture from people wanting a house with a white picket fence to dreaming of fame or hoping to marry a millionaire. It's impossible to say for certain why this has happened. I'd love to blame it entirely on reality TV. But surely the lack of obvious imagery around a middle-class life makes it harder to envision and thus desire this status.

The dream of great wealth for yourself, in lieu of shared prosperity and broad economic security for all, makes for fun movie plots. But as a national ethic, it's deeply disturbing. It's what allows conservatives to rail against an inheritance tax that affects merely 0.3 percent of our population and have the vast majority whose families will have nothing taxable to leave them nodding along in rabid disdain. It lends credibility to arguments about CEOs deserving their unprecedented compensation packages and year-end bonuses no matter the performance they've delivered. Because too many not only look up to the richest but also fantasize they too will join their ranks, it's all too easy to twist policies for shared contribution into seeming like singling out the best for punishment.

WE'RE US, NOT OTHER

If you've any lingering doubts that, as I've so helpfully summarized it, words mean things, consider the collaboration among a host of progressive activists that since early 2010 calls itself "the other 98%."[32]

Likely you haven't heard this message or think you're seeing a typo. This group assembled with a clear-cut agenda against corporate domination of elections, concerns for people facing foreclosure and contending with unemployment, and a desire to end tax giveaways for those who don't need them. Since the group's initial Tax Day Rally in 2010, it boasts nearly 150,000 likes on Facebook.

Enter Occupy Wall Street with what seems like an identical message and a one numeral difference, "the 99%." In fact, while the percentage point that separates these two similar themes may be of some importance; I'd argue it's the "other"

Source: John Sellers and Andrew Boyd.

in the name that hampered earlier efforts. It's tough to quantify influence on political beliefs and popular sentiment, but
this younger effort has double the number of Facebook fans—
and that's on just one of its many pages.

Defining the vast majority of Americans as *other* lends a
strange power to the super-elite. It becomes the standard, the
norm to which we're compared. Instead, as Occupy Wall
Street aptly illustrated, the plutocrats are the aberration that's
a danger to us all.

Further, the Other 98%'s slogan, "Democracy for the rest
of us," is troubling. For democracy to apply in some cases but
not all, even if it's 98 percent of situations, is to eliminate the
meaning of the term altogether. It's akin to "justice for some."
Democracy must offer everyone's voice a part in the choir.

By unifying nearly all under the banner of the 99%, it becomes meaningful to fight for an economy that works for
America. We're conveying, without needing to assert, that
we're the ones who matter. When we get into the business of
defining identity—as we saw with the study asking people
about being voters—we can connect powerfully. Words really
do matter, even seemingly harmless ones like *other* that unwittingly separate us from the cause we support.

CHAPTER 6

The Audacity of Audacity

A talent for speaking differently, rather than for arguing well, is the chief instrument of cultural change.
—RICHARD RORTY, *CONTINGENCY, IRONY, AND SOLIDARITY*

Our language needs to change and fast. If we don't establish and reaffirm the economy is something people made and continue to create, we're hard-pressed to get Americans to believe it can be fixed and made better by people. If we don't tell an accurate tale about what catalyzed the current recession, we're not adequately setting the stage for our calls for meaningful oversight. And if we fail to insist that what separates the rich from the rest is not their superiority but rather the policies they pay politicians to create and perpetuate, we're enabling the it's-your-own-damn-fault mentality that keeps us from doing right by all of our people.

But there's only so much even the most careful attention to evoking the right metaphors and avoiding the wrong frames can do. It's only in the perfume industry that the bottle itself can sell the product. You need to have a plot and credible characters to craft a compelling story line—no matter how great a writer you are. To describe the great possibilities a new kind of capitalism could bring, we'd need to know what that new kind of capitalism is. In other words, we have to stop contenting ourselves with asking for incremental change at the margins.

Leading progressive economists have offered up many of the pieces we need. Novel ideas like promoting shorter work-weeks, bringing the Fed under control, and growing the clean energy sector are paths toward the economy we would want. But many mysteries remain.

How, for example, do we assure growth and sustainability in a U.S. economy built on consumer spending? Or if growth is no longer our goal, what is, and what better future does it offer? How do we wrestle with the limitations of an America-first-and-sometimes-only mind-set, recognizing that while many of our countrymen are deeply hurt by free trade, so too are their counterparts across distant borders?

In the pages that follow, we'll return to what's inhibiting an honest accounting of the flaws in our current economic setup and what we would need to do to address them. This has much to do with the limitations of the field of economics it-self. Yet at the same time, there are incredible new ideas coming from creative economists. For each one, the now familiar issues of conceptual metaphor, framing, and passive voice threaten to impede our advocacy on their behalf, unless we change the language we use.

Implementing any one, and dare I dream all, of these recommendations would go a long way toward righting our economy by placing people at the forefront. Improving many lives and livelihoods, putting these new ideas in place would have the beneficial side effect of stabilizing and strengthening the economy.

At the same time, these policy suggestions, even taken together, lay bare the striking limits of our economic plan for the future. These are amazing ideas—legions ahead of where most of our politicians and business leaders are in their thinking about what's possible and how to legislate our way to a better America. And still, they don't add up together to a full vision of how our economy can and should function. They not only don't answer the big questions I've raised time and again in this book; they also don't really take up this critical task.

In reality, right now there's no consensus or simply very little even said on how to structure consumption, production, investment, compensation, and so on. These are the questions we *must* begin asking; the answers to them are long overdue.

WE HOLD THESE TRUTHS TO BE SELF-EVIDENT

As I've taken no pains to hide, I firmly believe our prevailing understanding of economics is inadequate. That may be putting it too mildly—I'd go so far as to say the discipline is deeply flawed. In fact, many in the profession will tell you this very thing even as they make their living continuing to study, teach, and publish within these skewed parameters.

Gregory Mankiw, the Harvard economics professor subjected to the student walkout in protest of his purported attachment to conservative economic assumptions described in Chapter 1, cuts straight to the heart of why economics can create models and offer insights but never fully answer policy questions. *New York Times* journalist David Segal illustrates this by analyzing an issue brought up at the outset from Mankiw's widely used *Principles of Economics* introductory textbook:

> A town must maintain a well. Peter, who earns $100,000, is taxed $10,000, or 10 percent of his income, while Paula, who earns $20,000, hands over $4,000, or 20 percent of her income.
>
> "Is this policy fair?" Mr. Mankiw asks in "Principles." "Does it matter whether Paula's low income is due to a medical disability or to her decision to pursue an acting career? Does it matter whether Peter's high income is due to a large inheritance or to his willingness to work long hours at a dreary job?"
>
> *Economics, Mr. Mankiw concludes, won't tell us,* definitively, whether Peter or Paula is paying too much, *because an answer inevitably leads to matters of values*, which inevitably leads to different answers.[1]

Theoretically, Mankiw is right. Examining fluctuations in and interaction between capital and labor, the two components of any economy, could be a value-neutral proposition. But unlike the hard sciences it aspires to emulate, economics describes and thus circumscribes the realm of human activity, organization, interaction, and needs. If there's a more value-driven undertaking, I'm not sure what it is.

In practice, as we've seen, the ways we speak about the economy and its related parts very much determine what we believe ought to be done about each. Nowhere does more of this talk happen than in the field that purports to study—according to Mankiw, somehow suspended outside questions of right and wrong—the economy. In short, the notion of some neutral, nonideological, purely descriptive observation and prediction scheme is ludicrous. The mere act of telling us who does what to whom with which resources transmits, if not overtly than unconsciously, judgment about the how these acts ought to transpire.

Whether Mankiw is actually unaware that his work is supersaturated with expectation and ideology or just pretending this is the case, a cursory examination of the so-called principles of his profession reveals a thought process dependent upon ideas so clearly off base, they veer into the ridiculous.

If you've suffered through a course on basic economics, you may recall the four assumptions at the heart of classic theory. These are delivered generally right after you get the syllabus and (hopefully) before you start texting with your friends or nodding off to sleep. If you've managed to avoid encountering or have forgotten these "rules," here's a refresher. It'll be over quickly, I promise.

1. Scarcity: the recognition that resources aren't infinite. Here, I'm completely with the economists. But this is about all I buy of the premise.

2. Nonsatiation: the idea that each of us has an infinite desire to consume anything and everything. (There's no limit to the number of televisions or toasters we want.) We never get full, and we can always have another round.

3. Perfect information: the assumption that producers and consumers all possess the same, complete information about every exchange and potential transaction. No one withholds key information—say, in pages of fine print or incomprehensible acronyms—for his or her own benefit.

4. Rational choice: the notion that producers and consumers act only to maximize their happiness (known as utility in economics). They are able to weigh their preferences about the infinite set of goods in their economic universe, and these preferences remain stable over time.

How well do these rules describe the world as it is? Perhaps slightly better than the Looney Tunes scenes of the coyote suspended in the air until he realizes he's run off a cliff accurately depict the workings of gravity on earth.

Refreshingly, these assumptions seem as absurd to lots of economists as, I'm hoping, they seem to you. Perfect information doesn't apply when you're selecting a babysitter for an infant who can't tell you how it went, nor does it hold if you fulfill the unfortunate stereotype of woman who knows nothing about cars getting fleeced by a shady mechanic. I don't suggest that all or even most economists believe these claims apply in all cases—just that they are applied as useful shorthand for modeling and predicting human behavior.

Volumes have been written about the fallacy of this so-called General Equilibrium Theory, also named, presumably without intended irony, General Welfare Theory. In fact, there are whole subdisciplines devoted to explaining what happens when these assumptions don't hold. Newer fields like behavioral economics incorporate the best thinking about human psychology and decisionmaking, attempting to improve the discipline. These advances are wonderful and welcome.

Even so, that these assumptions have been turned into ironclad rules hurts not only our understanding of economics but also our handling of the economy. And, worse yet, they undermine our belief in any collaborative endeavor, namely, democracy.

Dismal though it may be, economics has desired to call itself a science. And vying to be worthy of this designation, it has turned what are handy shortcuts for calculating and graphing human behavior into absolute truths. If we doubt people want to consume without limit and possess all information about their transactions, why do we believe in the complex models and conclusions that stem from these claims?

The assumptions behind microeconomic theory boil down to two things: (1) scarcity and (2) competition. The pleasure of giving things away, participating in clothing exchanges, and doing-it-yourself don't exist according to economics. Wikipedia makes no sense, Freecycle™ is a fiction, anonymous philanthropy never happens, and so on.

But far worse than getting wrong the story about how real people produce, consume, save, and invest, economics has helped cement the idea that you're on your own and the pickings are slim. There is no room for collaboration or deliberate choice to give more than you'll get (because you know this is the only way to get more than you gave).

These "rules" aren't just a way to contemplate human behavior; they've taken on the mantle of natural law. An apple falls on your head; that's gravity—the basis of physics. You always want to have that apple; that's fantasy—the basis of economics.

Hey, some of my best friends are economists. The kind who don't believe in a free and unfettered market (or would like to actually witness one without government subsidizing and propping up the rich). But even in this, they are usually advocating for "corrections" to the market, a balancing or softening of the full force of capitalism as we know it.

While I would go further than that, even with the changes I'd like to see implemented, I'm not making an argument for control over the means of production or for state intervention in distribution and ownership rights. I'm saying that the belief that we are all competing with each other for scarce resources, that life is by nature is a zero-sum game, ignores critical truths that deserve the mantle of "natural law" far more than the assumptions we've elected to believe.

Humans are a social species. We are pack animals; we like to be together lots of the time. We allow others to hold and care for our young. Some of our greatest joys and deepest cultural practices involve sharing: our homes with a visiting stranger, bread and wine with our friends, grief with our family members.

Competition and scarcity may exist in certain realms and regions—we have certainly done our best to make these notions into our reality. But more true, and certainly more natural, is our need and desire to make living in close quarters work. Most of us have agreed our best shot at this is through democratically elected government, laws, social supports, and mutual respect. These are the needs that cannot be satiated, and this is the information we should attempt to perfect.

Thus, we are long overdue for a serious debate about what the economy is, how it works, and, most importantly, what it exists to do for us. The assumptions at the heart of prevailing economic theory, no matter how much more sophisticated practitioners question and tweak them, pervert our ability to consider what we really want to get done. More precisely, they blind us to the fact that we generally refuse to conduct this conversation.

Nevertheless, there are some strikingly great suggestions coming from contemporary economists. Four policies in particular pose interesting strategies for restructuring tired old institutions and processes. Though they are far from the only fresh ideas enlivening economic debate, I hope these representative ideas give a glimpse into what could be possible if we got serious about making our economy work for us, instead of assuming it can only be the other way around. These are first steps toward the audacity of thought, vision, and word I'd like to see us come to embrace for ourselves, our economy, and our country.

FOUR ECONOMIC POLICIES THAT PROMOTE PEOPLE AND PLANET

While I've already alluded to some basic improvements I think are long overdue—paid family leave, for example—the suggestions below fall, for me, into a different category. These represent much-needed steps toward rethinking just how we determine fundamentals in our economy, like assigning monetary value to professions, increasing the number of levers we have to deal with inequality, and wrestling with our legacy of promoting homeownership even as we admit this isn't attainable, or even desirable, for all.

Create Less Work for Each, More Work for All

It's news to no one that there isn't enough work to go around right now. Recent rosier reports notwithstanding, our jobless figures have been high for so long that many folks who should be counted in these rates are keeping them artificially low by no longer looking for regular employment. And then there are those who are underemployed, taking whatever piecemeal hours they can manage to bring in some income.

On the whole, there are two ways of tackling this problem: increase demand for labor or divide up existing demand differently so that more people reap the benefits of accessing a portion of it. So far, we've focused only on the former. At least among those of us who have accepted the need for deliberate action to address our lack of jobs at all. The second idea has mostly not even come up for discussion.

Center for Economic and Policy Research co-director Dean Baker offers up a novel solution to this, outlined in many articles and most thoroughly in his recent book, *The End of Loser Liberalism*. He explains, "In the absence of a growing demand for labor that would increase employment, an alternative route is to divide up the existing work among more workers." Baker highlights the success of Germany in employing this approach during the recent downturn and boasting as a result, he contends, much less gloomy unemployment figures despite less than stellar growth of the overall economy.[2]

The idea here is to combine some portion of salary with unemployment benefits for hours that fall short of full-time employment. While this would require changes to how benefits are calculated and doled out, there's no need for any new government agencies or serious legislative novelty.

Admittedly, this approach would introduce new complexities for employers, and especially payroll managers, to handle. But it offers the morale-boosting benefit of avoiding layoffs. Unlike Mitt Romney, most of us don't feel comfortable with or excited about firing people. And even those who do get some kick out of this know that it harms overall productivity as it creates a noxious work climate.

Why is this policy with minimal to no fiscal impact a hard sell? Beyond the fact that you've likely not ever heard of it, the idea of working *less* is anathema to the very core of our economic assumptions. As we've seen with the deeply embedded notion of the economy as an enforcer of morality, there are *good* people who work hard and *bad* ones who don't. This kind of mixing them together to create some middle ground muddles the comfort of our reliable black-and-white thinking.

In fact, Baker, in describing his plan, inadvertently gives us a clue to what makes work sharing hard to get behind: "Work sharing might be a proper route back to full employment, since there is nothing written in stone about the current length of the work week or work year."[3] While there may not be a number of hours carved into tablets, there is very much an idea of how much each person should work: lots and lots and then some unpaid overtime for good measure.

As we saw, even staunchly progressive groups have joined conservatives in waving the "work hard" flag. A policy that's perceived as allowing—even facilitating—less effort from individuals doesn't compute in a thought system that asks each of us to put in as many hours as possible for our economy. Work sharing privileges *people's* needs before those of the economy. It matters little whether the actual effects on the economy, even in the damaging growth-obsessed ways we measure them today, are positive.

Currently in our society, not having a job is regarded as a good reason to be turned down for a job. Respected private sector employers, like Sony Ericsson, have blithely enacted policies to not hire the unemployed.[4] There's an unspoken belief behind these kinds of rules: U for "unemployed" is our modern-day Scarlet Letter. What will come next? Will not having eaten become grounds for refusing to feed people? It's hard to imagine, given this, how we'd get broad adoption for the idea of work sharing—even as the Obama administration included it in the Middle Class Recovery Act.

Until we reorient away from the economy as a moral enforcer and our admiration for hard work above and to the exclusion of such activities as raising our children or just simply relaxing with friends, real conversation about how to divvy up what's to be done—let alone how to compensate people for it—will elude us.

Base What You Owe in Student Loans on What You Make

Student debt now approaches $1 trillion. According to the Department of Education, over the last decade the average debt per student rose more than 50 percent, even after the numbers are adjusted for inflation.[5] This is where most market watchers would place their bets for the source of the next, seemingly inevitable financial bubble. Just as overvaluing homes helped make the mortgages on them become impossible for us to repay, default is the obvious next step as the tangible "worth" of higher education keeps diminishing. If you can't get a job after graduation, the much-touted income boost from a college or graduate degree disappears. Add to the things you can't afford as a new graduate the cost of the education you already purchased.

Although in 2009 Congress passed legislation to peg what someone owes on federal loans to a percentage of that person's income, the real reform not even on the table would force *private* lenders to set up the same system. Robert Reich has long championed this plan, shorthanded as income-based repayments (IBR). Commenting on National Public Radio years ago he said, "[The high earner who] landed that private-equity job would pay 10 percent of his income for 10 years, which would be a hefty sum. My students who go into social work or become artists would pay 10 percent of theirs, which would be far less. The private-equity guy would, in effect, subsidize the social worker and the artist."[6]

Reich's argument is that people should pursue their passions without undue regard for how to pay the piper for this after the fact. Hard as this idea is to incorporate into our present-day work-for-the-economy mentality, there's actual value to people doing what they love. More pragmatically, many much-needed professions that require extensive and expensive training really don't pay all that much.

Take, for example, medicine. High-paying specialties like dermatology or plastic surgery promise practitioners big bucks and thus are a fairly easy route to paying off debts incurred in training to earn them. But America desperately needs more primary care doctors, nurses, and physicians' assistants. And there's little to be made, especially considering what graduates owe back in loans, in these occupations.

There are countless careers integral to the basic functioning of our society that are not compensated commensurate with the value they generate. Education, social work, policy analysis, just to name a few, are among professions that generally require a bachelor and a master's degree but don't pay nearly enough to make obtaining either financially possible for most Americans.

At this point, I'm sure you have no trouble guessing the nature of opposition to this approach. One angry blogger spelled it out, after calling Reich's commentary a "whinatorial": "So let's see: We'll create an incentive for people to run up huge college loans pursuing whatever they like for as long as they like, knowing that they won't really have to pay it all back.

And they'll be subsidized by those who, instead of pursuing their whimsy, opt to take up well-paying jobs."[7]

Here we are back in the familiar conservative territory of moral order. The all but overt idea spelled out in these words is that there are good people who do what the economy demands and earn the big bucks. Penalizing them for the ridiculous whimsy of their inferior peers just distorts the entire system.

What this writer fails to grasp is that it's not just that we're prohibiting people from following their bliss; we're also designing a future where no one will want to do anything but be a banker, an engineer, or a corporate attorney. These jobs are fine, but we can't have a national economy where this is all college-educated people do.

But, again, this argument is one we're hard-pressed even to make. Within a framework of the economy as nature's mechanism to ensure profit, we can't have a coherent debate about what "society" needs. As Margaret Thatcher famously insisted, "There's no such thing as society." I would add, there's not even such things as people's needs or desires in a worldview where the economy comes first, last, and only.

We can't think ahead, plan, and steer toward a desirable course until we cement the notion that the economy is something under our power. Reich's plan is one commendable example of a policy that requires we understand our relationship to the economy very differently.

Ensuring the Right to Live in Your House

Foreclosure does far more than kick a family to the curb, if that's not bad enough to warrant our attention. It hastens the destruction of neighborhoods with blight and crime, brings down surrounding property values, *and* costs lenders handsomely. It's hard to imagine a bigger lose-lose proposition. Yet most mortgage holders continue to refuse—despite federal programs urging them to do so—to help people stay in their homes.

Enter the policy known as "right to rent." Another brainchild of Dean Baker, endorsed by minted conservative Andrew Samwick, Bush Jr.'s head of the Council of Economic Advisors. Partisan political magazines the *National Review* and the *American Prospect* may have hit a first with this one: both wrote in favor of it.

The basic idea is this: after receiving a foreclosure notice, you would have twenty-five days to go to court to ask for the right to rent your home for up to five years. The court would determine the fair-market rental price provided you meet certain eligibility requirements.

As a bonus, since banks don't want to play Mr. Farley to anyone's Jack Tripper, this will incentivize them to do what they ought to and work with owners to modify mortgages. It also buys owners time to find other more affordable housing or land work that would enable them to pay rent on another place or their old mortgage.

Arianna Huffington, in praising the idea, wrote, "It would be great to see that cleverness on a national scale—and quickly—because it's clear that the foreclosure crisis and the misery it brings won't be ending any time soon. . . . As many as 10 million of the 55 million outstanding mortgages in the U.S. are likely going to default. Those are devastating numbers." Not surprisingly, she employed the vehicle metaphor to conclude her editorial, saying, "So the question is: will our leaders—either political or business—take the wheel and turn it before we hit the iceberg?"[8]

The Right to Rent Act of 2010, sponsored by Representative Raul Grijalva (D-AZ) and Marcy Kantur (D-OH), languished in the House Finance Committee. Hopefully, we'll see it pass in the 2012 session, as legislators plan to reintroduce it.

You'll not be surprised to hear that our largest banks and mortgage institutions fought the plan all along. Obviously, their real reasons for doing so, concern over their mighty profits, don't make for good ad copy. So instead, they and their friends in conservative economic think tanks trotted out the idea of moral hazard.

In brief, allowing naughty defaulting homeowners to wind up anywhere other than the street (never mind the fact that they would be made to *pay*) is encouraging the very worst behavior. We'll have mass defaults as a result.

Even a cursory review of this concern proves its absurdity. Renting your own home, when you used to own it and presumably built up equity, is not much of a prize. Further, it asks nothing of taxpayers and adds zero to the all-important deficit.

More telling, however, is the response of the realtor community to this idea. Basically, criticism of it lands squarely in the vein of government involvement in private contracts equals socialism. As Matthew Ferrera, writing on his professional realtor advice blog, puts it, "Any plan that begins by abrogating the rights of mortgage holders to receive their assets back when borrowers cannot make their payments and dispose of it as they see fit is, by any other name, nationalization of the housing market."[9] Once again, we see aversion to the notion of anything in the economy requiring deliberate outside control. These realtors seem to have forgotten that without government—in the form of our courts—private contracts like mortgages are unenforceable and thus meaningless.

Make Manufacturing Inequality Expensive

The *New Republic*'s Mark Schmitt, in introducing the final "big" economic reform idea I long to see become law, succinctly lays out the contrasting views on the purpose of the economy I've been describing. Here they are, in his words, as pertaining particularly to our tax code: "If and when the tax reform moment arrives, you're guaranteed to hear two principles tossed around a lot. One is that we should have a 'clean' tax code that *doesn't try to 'pick winners' through narrow deductions and credits*. The other is that *we should 'tax what we want less of, and not what we want more of.'* That second principle conflicts with the first, since it implies picking winners."[10]

Schmitt packs a great deal into this passage. First, no matter how much certain people buy into the notion of the economy as best off just doing its own thing, this is a farce. As an entity deeply altered by human decisions, economic policy-making—in this case the tax code—will always guide how the economy and actors within it behave.

Second, the desire to cling to an ideal—in the face of all evidence to the contrary—of some kind of economic purity has become like an addiction for people who fall prey to it.

Look at the wording—"*clean* tax code," in particular. This suggests there's some kind of unsullied, natural state for this economic component. Deliberate planning to, horror of horrors, make things that are good for society and people pay off is not the place of the government. As we've seen, the magical market handles this on its own.

Schmitt then describes a tax code change to reduce something we really don't want: inequality. His idea is far more ingenious than standard approaches like increasing the earned income tax credit or restoring the top brackets to the wild hippie days of Ronald Reagan or Dwight Eisenhower. Both of which, don't get me wrong, are also stellar ideas.

But these are redistribution schemes. As Schmitt argues, "Taxation-as-redistribution treats inequality as if it were a natural fact, and then expects taxes to compensate for it. But inequality is the result of a lot of deliberate choices, especially decisions by companies about how to allocate revenues, and the tax code itself is responsible for many of them."[11] Sound familiar?

Here comes an approach to forcing elites to pay up for their actions. This, for me, is the policy equivalent of banishing gap language from our vocabulary in order to embrace the idea of human-made barriers. Although I take issue with his employing unhelpful metaphors, the proposal he summarizes is right on target: "Imagine a tax code that tried to undo its own damage. When so much inequality is created within single companies, why not reward companies that are narrowing the gap and tax companies that widen it? . . . [A proposal by] investor Steve Silberstein would adjust the corporate tax rate based on the ratio of CEO pay to the average worker."[12]

It's hard to imagine a more elegant answer to such a thorny problem. Pegging the corporate tax rate to corporate compensation policy preserves the precious freedom of the private sector. Businesses can pay what they like to all employees. But they can't continue, as many companies do now, to pay more in CEO salary than they do in annual taxes.

If they want to leave compensation for the big boss at current ridiculous levels, and in so doing screw the majority of their workers, it's their prerogative. But when said workers then must turn to public dollars for necessities like subsidized loans for their kids' educations or health care for themselves, we expect those same corporations to be putting into the pot for the things salaries should rightly cover—at least for a business that's doing so well it can afford to create Olympic-size swimming pools of cash for its top executives to get naked and swim in.

THESE FOUR PROPOSALS are all worth passing yesterday. But even they, and the handful of other great ideas that belong in this category, don't amount to an overall vision for how our economy ought to be working. Still, they represent the type of bold approach we should embrace. And they all, not coincidentally, rely upon the idea of the economy as something we made that should be working for the majority of us.

Ideally, the courage of these economic policies would fortify us to beef up how we talk about the economy and thus what we're willing and able to purpose for the American people. Thus, I turn now, in conclusion, to parting thoughts on the main topic I've taken up: communicating with deep clarity and effective audacity.

DON'T THINK OF AN ELEPHANT (UNLESS IT'S ABOUT TO TRAMPLE YOU)

In the years since the 2004 publication of George Lakoff's *Don't Think of an Elephant*, the progressive movement has become savvier about framing and marketing. But we haven't yet implemented the most important lessons his and related work offer about communicating clearly and well. And in some cases, we've embraced the opposite of what was intended. As the title of Lakoff's bestseller implies, asking people *not* to do something pretty much guarantees they will. Ask the parent of a teenager, or consider the fact that you bought this book in defiance of its title. The larger lesson is that when you try to speak against an idea by overtly referencing it, you make your audiences think precisely of it. When we say, for example, "Government is not the problem" or "Taxes are not a drain on the economy," we're speaking against our own positions.

These negative constructions give free airtime to our opponents' notions. Worse yet, they undermine our own. Even with perfect reading or audio comprehension (and recall, we're talking about our fellow Americans), our subconscious weights words differently. Whereas a noun like "government" or "taxes" stands out, a tiny word like "not" that offers no ready image goes by us, leaving the rest of the sentence foremost in our minds.

In outwardly asserting our negation, we bring our opinions to the rational minds of our audiences. They are now consciously contemplating, is what we claim true or isn't it? Do I believe this messenger or not? We would do well to exert less effort saying what we do not believe. It's a waste of our time, and as we know, airtime is hard to come by and eyeballs are distracted.

However, some have twisted this insight and cling to their misunderstanding of it quite fiercely. Many progressives have misinterpreted this otherwise sound messaging advice to believe not negating opposing frames means not criticizing our opponents. Or even mentioning them at all. Those seeking to derail our economy and block most of us from prosperity become Those Who Shall Not Be Named.

Case in point, as we've seen here in depth, is our reluctance to name names behind our present recession. "Mistakes were made," and "regulations were dismantled"—the closest we get to wagging our finger involves long paragraphs in the passive voice.

In the midst of stumbling over ourselves to be fair and accurate, we even manage to obscure what we actually believe. Consider, for a moment, an example from another important issue area: the debate over a woman's right to reproductive health services. Since *Roe* the dominant note we have sounded about abortion is one of "choice" and of keeping laws off our bodies. From arguing the landmark 1973 Supreme Court case on privacy, not equity, grounds, to pasting bumper stickers on our cars today, we took the libertarian approach, hoping to hook folks from the red side of the spectrum.

"My child, my choice." We claimed we wanted government out. And now it is. The absence of a federal mandate for insurance to cover abortion, the Hyde Amendment banning federal monies for abortion, and Republicans' successful attempts to defund Planned Parenthood all are aided by the effectiveness of that strategy.

It was never true that government had no role to play in women's reproductive care. We were deliberately not conveying our true feelings or values when we said "U.S. out of my uterus" and other things like it. Without government to help train new obstetricians at public medical schools and to ensure access to the procedure for all women, abortion has become—for many—a right we can't exercise. According to the Guttmacher Institute, as of the most recent data collection, it's impossible to get an abortion in 87 percent of U.S. counties. So much for our hard-fought choice.

Appealing to where (we think) people are has become the norm among progressives, especially as we've become evermore wedded to the proclamations of pollsters. This is what gives rise and lends credence to unhelpful slogans like "Work hard and play by the rules." Since people are afraid of terrorists, let's call our climate change efforts an antiterrorism program. Since people don't want to shell out for art programs in schools, let's tout how knowing music correlates to good math performance.

Unfortunately, as we've seen time and again, evoking our opponents' worldview in service of our policies only serves to push people further away from our beliefs. And, in turn, makes our policies seem less and less logical.

People may buy that foreign oil is a problem, but that doesn't help them understand why they shouldn't want to "Drill, baby, drill" in Alaska or forge the Keystone pipeline. Studies may convince them that music boosts math scores, but this just reinforces the assumption that the only thing that matters in school is arithmetic. As we've seen, they'll then choose to cut out the musical middleman.

When we take a "tax the rich" messaging approach to trying to rectify our deep and damaging inequality, we succeed at one thing for certain. We get people to hate paying taxes even more. Surely, this is a feat we should feel dubious about achieving.

Similarly, crying out about how "government failed" to regulate the financial industry makes our subsequent appeals for more government regulation sound ridiculous. Yet we often seem more comfortable crafting language from the underlying beliefs of our opponents than from our own.

In sum, it's not useful to "meet people where they are" if that place is destructive. We must instead borrow some gumption from our opponents, since as conservatives have proven time and again, it is possible to see where people are capable of going and to lead them there.

If we can learn anything from Republican messaging master Frank Luntz, it is to sing *our* fight songs and never mind about pissing off those who disagree with us. While progressives tread lightly and seek not to offend, conservatives turn the volume full blast on even the most outlandish of their opinions. They do not meet people where they are. They plant a flag where they'd like people to go and start a march there, without food or water, no matter the distance.

When they first introduced the idea of privatizing social security, for example, people recoiled. We forget, however, that conservatives expected that reaction. They did not ask their pollsters what people already endorsed at the time. They found some brave souls in their movement to be the right flank and say what was deeply unpopular at that moment. This way, each subsequent time they introduced the idea, it would sound less and less crazy. As a result, more "moderate" suggestions that wouldn't have even been up for debate a decade ago, like raising the retirement age and capping benefits, now sound like sensible centrism that Democrats should embrace before it's too late.

Here's another Republican secret: some of their leaders and figureheads will say ludicrous, offensive crap they know we will hate. This is red meat to the party faithful. As an added bonus, it repels us as progressives and might even make the mushy middle pay attention. The predictable result is that we then do them the huge favor of repeating what they've said over and over (and over)—gesturing wildly all the time and looking incredulous. Can you *believe* that he said that!?!?

Thus, we give them even more (free) airtime for their ideas. And when they introduce a slightly less extreme version of the same plan, it looks like a middle-of-the-road policy. This deliberate strategy is popularly called "Overton's Window" after the conservative academic who came up with it. By going way out, conservatives actually swing the pendulum of public opinion. And we help them out. Nudging ever closer to every new center, we shorten the bandwidth of political thought. What used to be left is now radical; ideas we would have called conservative are today labeled moderate.

Progressives could learn much from this strategy. Political communication expert and trainer John Neffinger tells a wonderful story to illustrate one of many opportunities we lost to employ it:

Not long after Bill Clinton's health care reform proposal went down to defeat in the Senate, Bill ran into Bernie Sanders, Congress's only avowed socialist. Bernie approached him with a grave look on his face. "Mr. President, I am so sorry. I failed you on health care."

Clinton was puzzled. Sanders had supported his reforms. "What do you mean, Bernie?" said Clinton. "You were with me every step of the way!"

"Exactly." replied Sanders. "I should have been burning you in effigy on the steps of the Capitol. Then people would have understood how moderate your plan really was."[13]

Sadly, for us, a "good" talking point generally means everyone kinda likes it. Democratic campaign strategists and even most progressives generally looking for something that polls well, like motherhood and apple pie, liberty for all. Please believe us: we're really reasonable people.

But as Ryan Clayton, a colleague in political advertising, illustrates in his carefully researched PowerPoint manifesto on immigration messaging, "Illegally Framed," a winning message is one that *engages the base*, *persuades the middle*, and *provokes the opposition* to reveal its true colors. We too need to offer red meat if we want the diehards in our movement to desire to repeat our messages.

Yes, it's true—everyone wants a free pony. If you try out that message, you'll register lots of approval. Unfortunately, we need to be marketing policies that ask folks to behave as adults. This is a long-recognized difference between a progressive platform and a conservative one that appeals to the basest desires for self first and foremost. Milquetoast appeals that mask what we need people to do and stop doing don't advance our actual policy objectives.

We see how far "the audacity of hope" took us; it's time now for the audacity of audacity. A real choir has many voice parts, including some way out at the far ends. Progressives must stop humming in a blandly nonoffensive alto. Regardless of what we do or say, our opponents will call us wildly out of touch and wacky, so we might as well have some fun and say what we actually mean. It's shockingly difficult for us to speak from our worldview, accustomed as we've become to walking the fictional middle line. We're losing so much ground in every battle, it feels scary to "go out on a limb" and come out swinging for what we believe. But make no mistake: continuing to do the same things and expecting different outcomes is a madness we don't have the time to indulge. Anyway, the public sees through us. When we say we want abortion because we oppose government interference or we want out of Afghanistan because it's too expensive, we double down on the ideas that government is bad and that death and destruction matter less than a bottom line. These are not our beliefs. We betray ourselves and look hollow and amoral to our audiences. Our words cannot stand up to the bright-line good-and-evil worldview our opponents convincingly feign. Saving money isn't much of a rejoinder to keeping America safe.

America and the world can't afford to have us keep remaking the communication mistakes of 2007. We lost our best moment to convince a public primed for an alternative vision for what the economy should be like. Even so, there's still enough demand for a coherent storyline that ours could break through. This would require that we have one. That's why it's time to get on metaphor and boldly describe the world we seek to inhabit with an economy working for all of us as a key component of it.

Acknowledgments

Like the proverbial horseshoe that saved the kingdom, a series of necessary but serendipitous connections made this book possible. My deep gratitude to Robert Kuttner for planting the idea of a book in my head and introducing me to Max Brockman, the agent who made it possible. Thanks also to his colleagues at Brockman Inc. for making the process for this first-time author so painless. Clara Platter brought me through the early stages of the process, having seen directions for the narrative even I didn't recognize. Brendan Proia took up the editorial helm and, through what I can only imagine amounted to criminal amounts of overtime, shaped the text into something clear, cogent, and persuasive. He made possible the completion of the manuscript by my nonnegotiable deadline: labor and delivery of my second child. Thanks as well to the whole team at PublicAffairs and Perseus, in particular Clive Priddle, Collin Tracy, and Jan Kristiansson, whose meticulous attention to detail (and dangling participles) made the text infinitely better.

An impressive cohort of scholars, activists, policymakers, and strategists offered up their insights and answered my (endless) questions despite other demands on their time. Thanks especially to Jenifer Fernandez Ancona, whose intellectual foresight and unwavering leadership on the issue of a progressive economic vision form the foundation of this book. Similarly, Barry Kendall helped propel the ideas contained within and later the actual content of the book with his timely, always insightful responses. Erica Payne made possible an integral component of the research that informs this book; she could teach a master class in speaking truth to power. Alongside these progressive leaders, I credit Ryan Senser, Billy Wimsatt, Rebecca Adamson, Sara Robinson, Anne Price, Van Jones, Chuck Collins, Drew Westen, Juhu Thukral, Dan Ancona, and David Atkins with improving the reach and clarity of my analysis. Some went above and beyond offering insights to take a hand in making critical suggestions on early drafts. To Ryan Clayton and Jenny Lederer, I owe way more than this written acknowledgment.

It was my immense fortune to encounter and work with my Real Reason cofounders Alyssa Wulf, Eric Sahlin, and Nancy Urban; they taught me the stuff of analysis and modeled for me courage, curiosity, perseverance, and attention to detail. If the ideas here offer any great insight or intellectual reach, it is only because they are built upon the strong foundations of the pioneering work of scholars I've had the enormous fortune to engage with firsthand: George Lakoff in the realm of cognitive linguistics, and Robert Reich, Steve Raphael, James Galbraith, and Elizabeth Warren in economics and public policy. Dean Baker also served as a key source of economic innovation and managed to find the time to review a chapter draft. As expected, any errors or omissions are entirely my own.

Writing a book while expecting and then caring for a newborn, not to mention working full-time, required the unwavering support of friends who stepped up at countless turns to make life more manageable. In particular, I feel inexplicably lucky to know and have the support of Julie Bannerman and Maya Delgado Greenberg—they are as great of friends as I could ever imagine. Despite their own familial and professional commitments, for helping encourage me no matter the hour and weigh in on key elements of the research and manuscript, I thank Elisabeth Hensley, Catherine Hazelton, Annette Doornbos, Sonia Pinto-Scherstuhl, Monica Long, Andy Greenstein, Jelena Simjanovic, Laura Paskell-Brown, Flora Hewlett, Samuel England, Roberto Hernandez, Layda Negrete, Joseph Reid, Ruti Zeligman, Regina Aguilar, Dana Hull, Keyvan Kashkooli, Jackie Downing, Rinat Fried, Sarah Berson, and Alysoun Quinby. Sita Davis played a dual role as both friend and photographer. My fellow Gan Avraham preschool parents kept me sane with meals and play dates; I thank Jill Lindenbaum, Rachel Dornhelm, Roberta Masliyah, Joel Mendelson, Jeanne Swartz, Mala Johnson, Hilary Altman, Alicia von Kugelgen, Kari Barnes, Jueli Garfinkle, and Carolyn Bernstein.

I owe my siblings (in blood and law) enormous gratitude for their patience, solicited opinions, and cheerleading. Dana Scheele and Ross Shenker may have no choice in their relation to me, but they always make the best of it. This applies also to my brother-in-law and writing buddy Todd Scheele. My other in-laws, Vilma, Glenda, Angelica, Armando, Jorge, and Juan Pablo Osorio, as well as Virgilia Garcia, have always been in my corner, even though I can't hand-press a decent tortilla. Factor in my parents, Lucyna and Yoram Shenker, and I have won the family lottery. They encouraged my unorthodox professional decisions, allowing me to pursue my interests and reassuring me it would all work out.

Finally, but really foremost, there aren't words in any language to properly acknowledge my husband, Donaldo Israel Osorio. Apart from being the greatest partner I could ever envision, he quietly models what it means to be progressive. *Yo sembrador(a) de ideas, tu sembrador de trigo*. For him and our children, Shai and Diego, I wrote this book in the hopes that it will offer some, albeit small, contribution to creating the world they deserve.

Notes

NOTES TO PREFACE: A FALSE IDOL

1. David Broder, "Sober Suggestions from Obama's Debt Commission," *Washington Post*, November 14, 2010, emphasis added.

2. Mitt Romney, campaign speech, Detroit, Michigan, February 24, 2012, emphasis added.

3. Tom Coburn, *Fox News Sunday*, December 26, 2010, emphasis added.

4. Jeb Hensarling, CNN, *State of the Union*, November 13, 2011, emphasis added.

5. John Boehner and Eric Cantor, "Mr. President, Let's Go to Work," *USA Today*, August 16, 2011, emphasis added.

6. See, among many reports and articles, Karen Campbell and James Sherk, "Extended Unemployment Insurance—No Economic Stimulus," Heritage Foundation, November 18, 2008.

7. Jeff Connaughton, "Obama and the Rule of Law," Huffington Post, December 19, 2011.

8. Quoted in Robert Kuttner, *Obama's Challenge: America's Economic Challenge and the Power of a Transformative Presidency* (White River Junction, VT: Chelsea Green, 2008).

9. Geraldine Ferraro, Speech at the Democratic National Convention, San Francisco, California, July 19, 1984.

10. Arnold Schwarzenegger, Speech at the Republican National Convention, New York, New York, August 31, 2004.

11. Van Jones is a former Obama Administration official and long-time social justice advocate, author of *Rebuild the Dream* (New York: Nation Books, 2012).

12. See "Contract for the American Dream" at www.rebuildthe dream.com.

13. Andrea Canning and Leezel Tanglao, "Ohio Mom Kelley Williams-Boler Jailed for Sending Kids to Better School District," *Good Morning America*, ABC News, January 26, 2011.

14. Linda Greenhouse, "Justices' Ruling Limits Lawsuits on Pay Disparity," *New York Times*, May 30, 2007.

15. Kevin Carson, "When You 'Work Hard and Play by the Rules,' the House Wins," Center for a Stateless Society, March 16, 2010.

16. ILO Report, cited in Steve Ashby, "Voice of the People," *Chicago Tribune*, September 15, 2011.

17. Coburn, *Fox News Sunday*, emphasis added.

NOTES TO CHAPTER 1: ONCE UPON OUR ECONOMY

1. Edmund Andrews, "Greenspan Concedes Error on Regulation," *New York Times*, October 23, 2008, emphasis added.

2. "Interest in Economic News Surges," Pew Research Center, October 1, 2008.

3. Roger Backhouse and Bradley Bateman, "Wanted: Worldly Philosophers," *New York Times*, November 5, 2011.

4. Ibid.

5. Jose DelReal, "Students Walk Out of Ec 10 in Solidarity with 'Occupy,'" *Harvard Crimson*, November 2, 2011.

6. Stephen Jay Gould, *Full House: The Spread of Excellence from Plato to Darwin* (New York: Three Rivers Press, 1997).

7. Paul Krugman, "Myths of Austerity," *New York Times*, July 1, 2010.

8. Paul Krugman, "The President Surrenders on Debt Ceiling," *New York Times*, July 31, 2011.

9. Bloomberg News National Poll, conducted by Selzer and Company, September 9–12, 2011.

10. Jim Zarroli, "Companies Sit on Cash; Reluctant to Invest, Hire," *All Things Considered*, National Public Radio, August 17, 2011.

11. Greg Sargent, "Americans Believe in the Confidence Fairy," *Washington Post*, September 14, 2011.

12. Eric Liu and Nick Hanauer, *The Gardens of Democracy: A New American Story of Citizenship, the Economy, and the Role of Government* (Seattle: Sasquatch Books, 2011).

13. Paul Krugman, "The Spiral of Inequality," *Mother Jones*, November/December 1996.

14. Barbara Ehrenreich, "This Land Is Their Land," *The Nation*, June 11, 2008.

15. Quoted in Jim Taylor, Doug Harrison, and Stephen Kraus, *The New Elite: Inside the Minds of the Truly Wealthy* (New York: Amacom, September 10, 1998).

16. Julia Isaacs, Isabel Sawhill, and Ron Haskins, "Getting Ahead or Losing Ground: Economic Mobility in America," Economic Mobility Project, February 20, 2008.

17. John Rawls, *A Theory of Justice* (Cambridge, MA: Belknap Press, 1971).

NOTES TO CHAPTER 2: WHAT WE'LL BUY ABOUT THE ECONOMY

1. Mackenzie Weinger, "Study: 8 in 10 Lawmakers Lack Education in Economics," *Politico*, August 23, 2011.

2. Annamaria Lusardi and Olivia Mitchell, "How Much Do People Know About Economics and Finance?," Policy Brief, University of Michigan Retirement Research Center, March 2008.

3. Findlaw.com survey, cited in "Two-Thirds of Americans Can't Name Any U.S. Supreme Court Justices, Says New FindLaw.com Survey," PR Newswire, June 1, 2010; Sam Dillon, "History Survey Stumps U.S. Teens," *New York Times*, February 26, 2008; "Young Americans Still Lack Basic Global Knowledge," National Geographic–Roper Survey, May 2, 2006.

4. Kristopher Gerardi et al., "Financial Literacy and Subprime Mortgage Delinquency," Working Paper, Federal Reserve Bank of Atlanta, April 2010.

5. See, among various available studies, Gene Amromin et al., "Financial Literacy and the Effect of Financial Counseling: A Review of the Literature," Federal Reserve Bank of Chicago, 2010.

6. "Many Americans Lack Basic Understanding of Finance," University of Cincinnati, Economics Center, November 14, 2010.

7. George Lakoff and Mark Johnson, *Metaphors We Live By*, 2nd ed. (Chicago: University of Chicago Press, 2003).

8. Paul Thibodeau and Lera Boroditsky, "Metaphors We Think With: The Role of Metaphor in Reasoning," *PLoS One*, February 23, 2011.

9. Robert Sapolsky, "This Is Your Brain on Metaphors," *New York Times*, November 14, 2010.

10. Frank Luntz, *Words That Work: It's Not What You Say, It's What People Hear* (New York: Hyperion Books, 2007).

11. "Estate Tax Myths," Center for Budget and Policy Priorities, revised February 23, 2009.

12. Lakoff and Johnson, *Metaphors We Live By*.

13. Cited in David Brooks, "Midlife Crisis Economics," *New York Times*, December 26, 2011.

14. "72% Favor Free Market Economy over One Managed by the Government," *Rasmussen Reports*, July 8, 2011.

15. Jeffrey Jones, "Americans Increasingly Prioritize Economy over Environment," Gallup Politics, March 17, 2011.

16. Nicole Gelinas, "Do What Most People Would Do with the Lottery Money," Room for Debate, *New York Times*, November 29, 2011.

17. Stephen Keen, "It's Time for a Pro-Growth Economic Policy," Heritage Foundation, March 4, 2009.

18. David Mason, "Avoiding a Keynesian Rush to Regulate the Financial Markets," Heritage Foundation, March 4, 2009, emphasis added.

19. Ibid., emphasis added.

20. Quoted in Tanya Somanader, "Is Senator Portman Open to Raising Revenue?," Think Progress, August 11, 2011, emphasis added.

21. Chris Edwards, "The Troubling Return of Keynesianism," CNS News, February 17, 2009.

22. Glenn Beck, Fox News, aired March 27, 2009, emphasis added.

23. Editorial, "Obama's Self-Immolating Capitalism," *The Week*, March 19, 2009.

24. Karen Campbell, "Time for Real Tax Change," *Front Page Magazine*, March 19, 2009.

25. Paul Krugman, "Revenge of the Glut," *New York Times*, March 2, 2009, emphasis added.

26. Ibid., emphasis added.

27. Ethan Pollack, "A Meaningful Stimulus for Main Street," Economic Policy Institute, October 22, 2008, emphasis added.

28. Sally Kohn, "Fixing the Economy Won't Fix Wall Street," AlterNet, September 19, 2008, emphasis added.

29. Tony Avrigan, "Economies of Major Developed Countries Will Shrink in 2009," Economic Policy Institute, February 18, 2009, emphasis added.

30. Cliff Hilton, "How Obama Should Fix the Economy," *CNN Money*, August 11, 2008.

31. John McCain, Speech at the Heritage Foundation, Washington, DC, March 26, 2009.

32. Henry Olsen and John Flugstad, "The Forgotten Entitlements," Hoover Institution, January 27, 2009, emphasis added.

33. Alan Reynolds, "Is Capitalism Dead? Yes," National Public Radio, March 11, 2009.

34. Matthew Continetti, "End Corporate Welfare," All Business, March 30, 2009, emphasis added.

35. Vicki Needham, "House Republicans Propose Drug Testing for Unemployment Benefits," *The Hill*, December 9, 2011.

36. David Edwards, "Florida's Welfare Drug Testing Costs More Than It Saves," Raw Story, August 9, 2011.

37. "Growing Support for Drug Testing of Welfare Recipients," Associated Press, February 25, 2012.

38. Suzanne Mettler, "Our Hidden Government Benefits," *New York Times*, September 19, 2011.

39. Binyamin Appelbaum and Robert Gebeloff, "Even Critics of the Safety Net Increasingly Dependent Upon It," *New York Times*, February 11, 2012.

40. Charles Murray, *Coming Apart: The State of White America, 1960–2010* (New York: Crown Forum, 2012).

41. Jim Wallis, "Budgets Are Moral Documents Part II," Huffington Post, March 9, 2007, emphasis added.

42. Robert Reich, "Does the Free Market Corrode Moral Character? We'd Rather Not Know," Templeton Foundation.

43. "Recovery and Reinvestment 101," Center for American Progress, January 28, 2009.

44. David Leonhardt, "Obamanomics," *New York Times*, August 20, 2008.

45. Barack Obama, Speech on the Better Building Initiative, Washington, DC, December 2, 2011.

46. Courtney Schlisserman and Shobhana Chandra, "U.S. Economy: Consumer Confidence Near a Record Low," Bloomberg, March 31, 2009.

47. Nick Hanauer and Eric Liu, "The Progressive Economy: A Primer on Complexity Economics, and a New Paradigm for Policy," Unpublished memo to the Democracy Alliance, February 2009.

48. Scott Martin, "It's Time to Soak the Poor," Conservatism Today, July 17, 2008, emphasis added.

49. "Green Collar Jobs Campaign, Green Partners," Ella Baker Center web page; "Recovery and Reinvestment 101."

50. Barack Obama, Speech in Osawatomie, Kansas, December 6, 2011, emphasis added.

51. Rania Khalek, "4 Desperate Ways the Hardest Hit Are Coping with Economic Crisis," AlterNet, August 18, 2011.

52. Robert Borsage, "Learning Deficits," Campaign for America's Future, March 25, 2009.

53. Mason, "Avoiding a Keynesian Rush."

54. Editorial, "Low Wage Workers in This Economy," *New York Times*, March 23, 2009.

55. Andy Clasper, "Rising Up to Heal a Sick Global System," *Sojourners*, March 23, 2009.

56. Editorial, "Obama's Self-Immolating Capitalism," The Week, March 19, 2009, emphasis added.

57. Peter Baker, "Familiar Obama Phrase Being Groomed as Slogan," *New York Times*, May 15, 2009.

58. Robert Reich, "Is Obamanomics Conservative or Revolutionary?," blog post, March 11, 2009, emphasis added.

59. Robert Reich, "Totally Spent," *New York Times*, November 3, 2008, emphasis added.

60. "A Statement to Support and Build upon President Obama's Budget Priorities," Rebuild and Renew America Now, April 21, 2009; Pinyo Bhulipongsanon, "Where to Find Small Business Loans," Moolanomy, October 8, 2008.

61. Franklin Delano Roosevelt, Speech at Oglethorpe University, Atlanta, Georgia, May 22, 1932.

62. Lawrence Mischel and Jeremy Irons, "EPI Statement on Economic Recovery Package," Economic Policy Institute, February 12, 2009, emphasis added.

63. Leonhardt, "Obamanomics," emphasis added.

64. Paul Krugman, "Who'll Stop the Pain?," *New York Times*, February 20, 2009, emphasis added.

65. Barack Obama, Speech in Toledo, Ohio, June 3, 2011.

66. Ibid.

67. Ibid.

NOTES TO CHAPTER 3: DON'T CALL IT A CRISIS

1. Based on State Department figures for 2011 passports in circulation and census data.

2. Mahmood Sariolghalam, "Justice for All," *Washington Quarterly*, Spring 2001.

3. Rick Santelli, "Rant," CNBC, February 19, 2009.

4. Quoted in Michael Powell, "Gilded Blinders to the Reality of a Collapse," *New York Times*, November 7, 2011.

5. Alex Pollock, "Ten Ways to Do Better in the Next Financial Cycle," *The American* (American Enterprise Institute), July 28, 2009.

6. George W. Bush, Speech in Kennesaw, Georgia, February 20, 2003.

7. Quoted in Alan Zibel, "Will the White House Move the 'Boulder' on Principal Write-Downs?," *Wall Street Journal*, January 31, 2012.

8. Joseph Stiglitz, "Anatomy of a Murder: Who Killed the American Economy?," *Critical Review* 21, nos. 2–3 (June 2009).

9. Carmen Reinhart and Kenneth Rogoff, *This Time Is Different: Eight Centuries of Financial Folly* (Princeton, NJ: Princeton University

Press, 2009); John Cassidy, *How Markets Fail: The Logic of Economic Calamities* (New York: Farrar, Straus and Giroux, 2009); Joseph Stiglitz, *Freefall: America, Free Markets, and the Sinking of the World Economy* (New York: Norton, 2010).

10. Quoted in Ezra Klein, "Blame People for the Financial Crisis," *Washington Post*, January 11, 2010.

11. This author spells his name with lowercase letters only.

12. john a. powell, "Poverty and Race Through a Belongingness Lens," Nonprofit Alliance of Monterey Web page, emphasis added.

13. Barry Reinholz, "What Caused the Financial Crisis? The Big Lie Goes Viral," *Washington Post*, November 5, 2011.

14. http://www.merriam-webster.com/dictionary/crisis.

15. This widely used phrase owes its more recent popularity most notably to Harvard law professor and candidate for the Senate Elizabeth Warren, who championed the creation of the newly established Consumer Protection Agency.

16. Paul Krugman, "Making Banking Boring," *New York Times*, April 9, 2009.

NOTES TO CHAPTER 4: DO YOU THINK THE POOR ARE LAZY?

1. Mathew Continetti, "About Inequality," *Weekly Standard*, November 14, 2011.

2. "A Deeper Look at Income Inequality," House Budget Committee Publications, Paul Ryan, Chairman, November 17, 2011.

3. Michael Norton and Dan Ariely, "Building a Better America One Wealth Quintile at a Time," *Perspectives on Psychological Science*, January 2011.

4. Quoted in "Cain Tells Wall Street Protesters: It's YOUR Fault You Don't Have Jobs," Fox News, October 5, 2011, emphasis added.

5. Quoted in Elicia Dover, "Gingrich Says Poor Children Have No Work Habits," ABC News, December 1, 2011.

6. Mathew Yglesias, "Mitt Romney Says Concern About Inequality Is Just 'Envy,'" *Slate*, January 12, 2012.

7. Gene Marks, "If I Was a Poor Black Kid," *Forbes*, December 12, 2011.

8. P. J. O'Rourke, "Closing the Wealth Gap," Cato Institute, June 11, 1997.

9. Ludwig von Mises, "Inequality of Wealth and Incomes," *Freedom Daily* (The Future of Freedom Foundation), October 1998, emphasis added.

10. Harold Meyerson, "Who's Hurt by Paul Ryan's Budget Proposal?," *Washington Post*, April 5, 2011.

11. http://the53.tumblr.com/.

12. Alexander Russo, "Reformaggedon," *This Week in Education*, December 14, 2011, emphasis added.

13. James Warren, "Economist's Plan to Improve Schools Begins Before Kindergarten," Chicago News Cooperative, December 23, 2010, emphasis added.

14. Michelle Alexander, *The New Jim Crow* (New York: The New Press, 2012).

15. "The Great Recession Exacerbated Existing Wealth Disparities," Economic Policy Institute, Press release, March 29, 2011.

16. Cited in Martin Haberman, "Teacher Burnout in Black and White," National Center for Education Statistics, Haberman Educational Foundation, 2004.

17. "The Impact of Food Insecurity on the Development of Young Low-Income Black and Latino Children," Research Findings from the Children's Sentinel Nutrition Assessment Program (C-SNAP), Prepared for the Joint Center for Political and Economic Studies Health Policy Institute, May 2006.

18. Sarah Fass and Nancy Cauthen, "Who Are America's Poor Children?," National Center for Children in Poverty, December 2006.

19. Robert Bullard, "More Blacks Overburdened with Dangerous Pollution," Environmental Justice Resource Center, December 19, 2005.

20. Neeraj Mehta, "Why Are People Poor?," *Star Tribune*, June 22, 2009.

21. Reproduced with permission from Alberto Alesina and George-Marios Angeletos, "Fairness and Distribution: US vs. Europe," Working Paper No. 02-37 (Cambridge, MA: Institute for Economic Research, Harvard University, 2003).

22. Robert Rector, "How Poor Are America's Poor? Examining the 'Plague' of Poverty in America," Heritage Foundation, August 2007.

23. Editorial, "The New (Improved) Gilded Age," *The Economist*, December 19, 2007.

24. Will Wilkinson, "Thinking Clearly About Income Inequality," Cato Institute, July 14, 2009.

25. James Twitchell, "Needing the Unnecessary," *Reason Magazine*, August/September 2002.

26. Rector, "How Poor Are America's Poor?"

27. David Frum, "The Vanishing Republican Voter," *New York Times*, September 7, 2008.

28. James Galbraith, "With Economic Inequality for All," *The Nation*, September 7–14, 1998.

29. Stephen Rose, "5 Myths About the Poor Middle Class," *Washington Post*, December 23, 2007.

30. Dick Armey, "Frankly Demagogic," *Washington Times*, March 9, 2007.

31. Wilkinson, "Thinking Clearly About Income Inequality."

32. Louis Uchitelle, "The Richest of the Rich, Proud of a New Gilded Age" *New York Times*, July 15, 2007.

33. Arianna Huffington, "Is *Undercover Boss* the Most Subversive Show on Television?," Huffington Post, March 8, 2010.

34. inequality.org; Gene Sperling, "Rising Tide Economic," *Democracy: A Journal*, Fall 2007.

35. Galbraith, "With Economic Inequality for All."

36. Insight Center for Community Economic Development, "Letter to Member of Congress on Tax Reform," November 12, 2010, emphasis added.

37. "NPR Blames Racism for Racial Wealth Gap, Ignores Role of Marriage," We the Conservatives, September 15, 2011.

38. Robert Rector, Kirk Johnson, and Patrick Fagan, "Understanding Differences in Black and White Poverty Rates," Heritage Foundation, May 23, 2001.

39. John Cavanaugh and Chuck Collins, "The Rich and the Rest of Us," *The Nation*, June 11, 2008.

40. Working Group on Extreme Inequality, inequality.org.

41. Ibid.

42. Tamara Draut, *Strapped: Why America's 20- and 30-Somethings Can't Get Ahead* (New York: Doubleday, 2006).

43. Mariko Chang, "Lifting as We Climb," Insight Center for Community Economic Development, Spring 2010.

44. Thomas Shapiro, Tatjana Meschede, and Laura Sullivan, "The Racial Wealth Gap Increases Four-Fold," Institute on Assets and Social Policy, May 2010.

45. Sarah Treuhaft, Angela Glover Blackwell, and Manuel Pastor, "America's Tomorrow: Equity Is the Superior Growth Model," PolicyLink, 2011.

46. Sally Kohn, "Stimulus for All," Huffington Post, January 14, 2009.

47. George Lakoff, *Moral Politics* (Chicago: University of Chicago Press, 1996).

48. Pam Fessler, "Making It in the U.S.: More Than Just Hard Work," National Public Radio, September 15, 2011.

49. Ayn Rand, *Atlas Shrugged* (New York: Penguin, 1957).

50. Jennifer Burns, *Goddess of the Market: Ayn Rand and the American Right* (New York: Oxford University Press, 2009).

51. Cavanaugh and Collins, "The Rich and the Rest of Us," emphasis added.

52. "A New Era of Promise: Renewing America's Responsibility," Office of Management and Budget, 2009.

53. Amaad Rivera et al., "State of the Dream," United for a Fair Economy, 2009.

54. O'Rourke, "Closing the Wealth Gap."

55. Kohn, "Stimulus for All," emphasis added.

56. Cavanaugh and Collins, "The Rich and the Rest of Us."

57. David Leonhardt, "In Health Bill Obama Attacks Inequality," *New York Times*, March 24, 2010.

58. "Unequal Starting Line," Institute for Policy Studies, YouTube video.

59. Draut, *Strapped*.

60. Kohn, "Stimulus for All," emphasis added.

61. Peter Schwartz, "In Defense of Income Inequality," *Tampa Tribune*, March 30, 2007, emphasis added; Dick Armey, "The 'War on Poverty' Turns 40," FreedomWorks, January 9, 2004, emphasis added.

62. john a. powell, "Poverty and Race Through a Belongingness Lens," Nonprofit Alliance of Monterey Web page, emphasis added.

63. Martin Luther King Jr., "I Have a Dream," Speech at the March on Washington, Lincoln Memorial, Washington, DC, August 28, 1963, emphasis added.

NOTES TO CHAPTER 5: WORDS MEAN THINGS

1. Christopher Bryan, Greg Walton, Todd Rogers, and Carol Dweck, "Motivating Voter Turnout by Invoking the Self," *Proceeding of the National Academy of Sciences*, June 22, 2011.

2. For more background, see Dean Baker, *The End of Loser Liberalism: Making Markets Progressive* (Washington, DC: Center for Economic and Policy Research, 2011); and Robert Reich, *Supercapitalism: The Transformation of Business, Democracy, and Everyday Life* (New York: Knopf, 2007).

3. Ben Protess, Michael de la Merced, and Susanne Craig, "Corzine-Led Firm Is Said to Be Eyed on Missing Money," *New York Times*, November 1, 2011, emphasis added.

4. John Schmitt, "Inequality as Policy: The United States Since 1979," *real-world economics review*, no. 51 (December 2009), emphasis added.

5. Devin Leonard, "All I Want in Life Is an Unfair Advantage," *CNN Money*, August 8, 2005.

6. Mariko Chang, "Lifting as We Climb," Insight Center for Community Economic Development, Spring 2010, emphasis added.

7. Thomas Shapiro, Tatjana Meschede, and Laura Sullivan, "The Racial Wealth Gap Increases Four-Fold," Institute on Assets and Social Policy, May 2010, emphasis added.

8. Meizhu Liu, "Letter to Congress on Tax Reform," November 12, 2010, emphasis added.

9. Mara Liasson, "Conservative Advocate," *Morning Edition*, National Public Radio, May 25, 2001.

10. http://www.riger.com/know_base/advertising/top_ten.html.

11. Ronald Reagan, "A Time of Choosing," televised speech, October 27, 1964, emphasis added.

12. Gerald Ford, Speech to Joint Session of Congress, Washington, DC, August 12, 1974.

13. Don Frederick, "John McCain and 'My Friends': We Count the Number of Times He Said It," *Los Angeles Times*, October 8, 2008.

14. Mitt Romney, Speech at the Iowa State Fair, Des Moines, Iowa, August 11, 2011.

15. Quoted in James Pethokoukis, "The Super-Risks of Taxing the Superwealthy," *U.S. News & World Report*, November 8, 2007.

16. Letter by Jude Wanniski in response to Paul Krugman's "The Spiral of Inequality," *Mother Jones*, January/February, 1997.

17. Peter Schwartz, "In Defense of Income Inequality," *Tampa Tribune*, March 30, 2007.

18. Michael Cox and Richard Alm, "Buying Time," *Reason Magazine*, August/September 1998.

19. Ludwig von Mises, "Inequality of Wealth and Incomes," *Freedom Daily* (The Future of Freedom Foundation), October 1998.

20. Dick Armey, "Frankly Demagogic," *Washington Times*, March 9, 2007.

21. Les Leopold, "Stimulus Versus Deficit Reduction? Wrong Debate," Huffington Post, November 30, 2009; Tamara Draut, *Strapped: Why America's 20- and 30-Somethings Can't Get Ahead* (New York: Doubleday, 2006).

22. Jim Carr, "An Equal Opportunity Recession," Reuters, March 15, 2009, emphasis added.

23. Robert Kuttner, "Rage the Left Should Use," *Washington Post*, August 18, 2009, emphasis added.

24. Amaad Rivera et al., "State of the Dream," United for a Fair Economy, 2009, emphasis added.

25. Chang, "Lifting as We Climb," emphasis added.

26. Women of Color Policy Network, "Disparities for Women of Color in Retirement," Testimony before the U.S. Department of Labor, ERISA Advisory Council, August 4, 2010, emphasis added.

27. "Diverging Pathways: How Wealth Shapes Opportunity for Children," Insight Center for Community Economic Development, 2011, emphasis added.

28. Chang, "Lifting as We Climb," emphasis added.

29. Meizhu Liu and Robert Clay, Letter to Jared Bernstein, Chief Economist and Economic Policy Advisor, Office of Vice President Joe Biden, Insight Center for Community Economic Development, November 8, 2010, emphasis added.

30. "Diverging Pathways."

31. "Defining the Middle Class," factcheck.org, January 24, 2008.

32. http://other98.com/.

NOTES TO CHAPTER 6: THE AUDACITY OF AUDACITY

1. David Segal, "The X Factor of Economics," *New York Times*, October 16, 2010, emphasis added.

2. Dean Baker, *The End of Loser Liberalism: Making Markets Progressive* (Washington, DC: Center for Economic and Policy Research, 2011).

3. Ibid.

4. Adam Cohen, "Jobless Discrimination? When Firms Won't Even Consider Hiring Anyone Unemployed," *Time*, May 23, 2011.

5. John Pulley, "The High Cost of Giving Back," *SSA Magazine*, Fall 2007.

6. Robert Reich, Commentary on *Marketplace*, National Public Radio, May 16, 2007.

7. "Robert Reich's Dumb Idea," Acumenicus, May 17, 2007.

8. Arianna Huffington, "Right to Rent: A Simple, Sensible Idea That Dysfunctional Washington Is More Than Happy to Let Die," Huffington Post, November 8, 2011.

9. Matthew Ferrera, "Realtors Beware: H.R. 5028 Could Collapse the Housing Market," mathewferrara.com, September 23, 2010.

10. Mark Schmitt, "How Tax Reform Represents Obama's Greatest Shot at Hope and Change," *New Republic*, July 24, 2011, emphasis added.

11. Ibid.

12. Ibid.

13. John Neffinger, "The 3 Lost Lessons of Healthcare History: Will Obama Re-learn Them in Time?," Huffington Post, September 6, 2009.

Index

SITA DAVIS

Anat Shenker-Osorio is a strategic communications consultant based in Oakland, CA. She crafts messaging for issues from immigration to contraception and, for the past three years, has extensively researched how people make sense of and come to judgments about the economy. Anat has worked with the ACLU, Ms Foundation, America's Voice, Ford Foundation, and dozens of others, presenting findings to members of Congress, and as a keynote speaker at Netroots Nation. This is her first book.

PublicAffairs is a publishing house founded in 1997. It is a tribute to the standards, values, and flair of three persons who have served as mentors to countless reporters, writers, editors, and book people of all kinds, including me.

I. F. STONE, proprietor of *I. F. Stone's Weekly*, combined a commitment to the First Amendment with entrepreneurial zeal and reporting skill and became one of the great independent journalists in American history. At the age of eighty, Izzy published *The Trial of Socrates*, which was a national bestseller. He wrote the book after he taught himself ancient Greek.

BENJAMIN C. BRADLEE was for nearly thirty years the charismatic editorial leader of *The Washington Post*. It was Ben who gave the *Post* the range and courage to pursue such historic issues as Watergate. He supported his reporters with a tenacity that made them fearless and it is no accident that so many became authors of influential, best-selling books.

ROBERT L. BERNSTEIN, the chief executive of Random House for more than a quarter century, guided one of the nation's premier publishing houses. Bob was personally responsible for many books of political dissent and argument that challenged tyranny around the globe. He is also the founder and longtime chair of Human Rights Watch, one of the most respected human rights organizations in the world.

$\cdot \quad \cdot \quad \cdot$

For fifty years, the banner of Public Affairs Press was carried by its owner Morris B. Schnapper, who published Gandhi, Nasser, Toynbee, Truman, and about 1,500 other authors. In 1983, Schnapper was described by *The Washington Post* as "a redoubtable gadfly." His legacy will endure in the books to come.

Peter Osnos, *Founder and Editor-at-Large*